Key French Grammar and Vocabulary

Heather Mascie-Taylor

Nelson

This book is intended as a reference and revision aid for students preparing for public examinations. The main points of French grammar are explained in clear and straightforward terms with examples from modern, everyday French. There has been no attempt to cover every possible detail nor to deal with minor exceptions to the main rules.

Thomas Nelson and Sons Ltd
Nelson House Mayfield Road
Walton-on-Thames Surrey
KT12 5PL UK

Nelson Blackie
Wester Cleddens Road
Bishopbriggs
Glasgow
G64 2NZ

Thomas Nelson (Hong Kong) Ltd
Toppan Building 10/F
22a Westlands Road
Quarry Bay Hong Kong

Thomas Nelson Australia
102 Dodds Street
South Melbourne
Victoria 3205 Australia

Nelson Canada
1120 Birchmount Road
Scarborough Ontario
M1K 5G4 Canada

© Heather Mascie-Taylor 1983

First published by E J Arnold and Son Ltd 1983
ISBN 0-560-00775-2

This edition published by Thomas Nelson and Sons Ltd 1989

I(T)P Thomas Nelson is an International
Thomson Publishing Company.

I(T)P is used under licence.

ISBN 0-17-439453-5
NPN 9 8

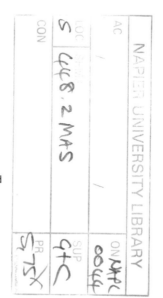

Printed in China

Contents

6 Adjectives

7 Adverbs

8 Negatives

9 Pronouns (subject and object)

10 *y* and *en*

Section B VOCABULARY

1   Introduction and definitions

Every subject has a certain number of technical terms and a language, such as English or French, is no exception. These technical or grammatical terms help to explain the rules and patterns of the language. The most commonly used ones are explained below.

Noun

A **noun** is the name of a thing, a person, an animal or a place. 'Passport', 'Philip', 'dog' and 'town' are all nouns in English, just as *un passeport, Philippe, un chien* and *une ville* are all nouns in French. The names of things you feel or experience are also nouns, such as 'friendship' *(l'amitié)*, 'luck' *(la chance)* and 'happiness' *(le bonheur)*.

Masculine and feminine

All nouns in French are either **masculine** or **feminine**. The article (the word for 'a' or 'the') will usually tell you the gender of a noun (whether it's masculine or feminine). Sometimes the ending of the noun will give you a clue about the gender, but in most cases, you just have to learn whether a word is masculine or feminine.

Masculine and feminine do not necessarily mean the same as male and female; for instance *une personne* is a feminine noun which could refer to a man as well as to a woman.

Singular and plural

A **singular noun** means that there is only one thing or person. In English, 'cat,' 'doctor' and 'house' are all singular nouns. Similarly in French, *le chat, le médecin* and *la maison* are also singular nouns. A **plural noun** means that there is more than one thing or person: 'books', 'tourists' and 'shops' are examples of plural nouns in English, just as *des livres, des touristes* and *des magasins* are plural nouns in French.

Article

The **definite article** is the word for 'the' which appears before the noun. *Le, la, l'* and *les* are all definite articles in French.

The **indefinite article** is the word for 'a' or 'an' which appears before the noun. *Un, une* and *des* are all indefinite articles in French.
In English, we often leave out the article, but it must never be left out in French (except in very rare cases).

Pronoun

A **pronoun** is used in place of a noun and saves you having to repeat the noun. 'He' *(il)*, 'him' or 'her' *(lui)*, 'we' or 'us' *(nous)* are all examples of pronouns.

Adjective

An **adjective** is a word which tells you more about a noun, e.g.

Paris is a beautiful and important city. Paris est une **belle** ville **importante**.

In the above example 'beautiful' *(belle)* and 'important' *(importante)* are adjectives. In French, adjectives agree with the noun, that is they are masculine, feminine, singular or plural to match the noun.

Verb

Every sentence contains at least one **verb**. Most verbs express action, e.g.

He buys some stamps. Il **achète** des timbres.

She went out. Elle **est sortie**.

Sometimes, verbs describe the state of things, e.g.

It was fine. Il **faisait** beau. *I have two brothers.* J'**ai** deux frères.

Verbs in French have different endings and forms depending on the person ('I', 'you', 'he', 'she' etc.), whether singular or plural ('I' or 'we', 'he' or 'they'), and the tense.

Regular and irregular verbs

Regular verbs follow a set pattern. For instance, the verb *travailler* follows the pattern of all regular -er verbs in French, just as *rendre* follows the pattern of regular -re verbs. **Irregular verbs** follow different patterns. Some of the most commonly used verbs in French are irregular, such as *avoir, être, faire* and *aller.* Some verbs are irregular in some tenses, but not in others.

Infinitive

The **infinitive** is the form of the verb which you would find in a dictionary. It means to do something, e.g. 'to have', 'to see'. Regular verbs in French have an infinitive which ends in -er, -re or -ir. Sometimes the infinitive of a verb is used with another verb in a sentence. The infinitive never changes form, e.g.

Je voudrais **passer** une semaine à Tours.

Dans le Val de Loire on peut **visiter** beaucoup de châteaux.

Reflexive verbs

Reflexive verbs are verbs which are used with a reflexive pronoun. They sometimes describe an action done to oneself, e.g.

Je **me lave**.	*I wash myself.*
Elle **se coiffe**.	*She combs her hair.*
Il **se couche**.	*He goes to bed.*
Nous **nous sommes reposés**.	*We had a restful (relaxing) time.*
Ils **se sont suicidés**.	*They committed suicide.*

In English, the reflexive pronoun ('myself', 'himself' etc.) is often not translated.
The infinitive of a reflexive verb in French always contains the reflexive pronoun, usually *se*, e.g. *se lever, s'habiller* etc., and this must never be omitted.

Tense

The **tense** of the verb tells you the time when something took place.

PRESENT TENSE:	Je **joue** au tennis.	*I'm playing tennis.*
PERFECT TENSE:	J'**ai joué** au tennis.	*I played tennis.*
IMPERFECT TENSE:	Je **jouais** au tennis (tous les jours).	*I used to play tennis (every day).*
CONDITIONAL TENSE:	(Si j'avais le temps,) je **jouerais** au tennis.	*(If I had time),* *I would play tennis.*
PLUPERFECT TENSE:	J'**avais joué** au tennis.	*I had played tennis.*

Auxiliary verb and past participle

Many past tenses, such as the Perfect and Pluperfect tenses, contain two parts to the verb: an **auxiliary verb** and a **past participle**. In French, the auxiliary (or helping) verb is part of *avoir* or *être*. The past participle is usually formed from the infinitive and ends in *é, i* or *u*. It gives the meaning of the verb, e.g.

Nous **avons commandé** le menu à prix fixe.	*We've ordered the fixed-price menu.*

In the above sentence, *avons* ('have') comes from the verb *avoir* ('to have') and is the auxiliary verb. *Commandé* ('ordered') is the past participle and adds the meaning.

Adverb

An **adverb** tells you more about the verb, often explaining *how, when* or *where* something happens. Many adverbs in English end in '-ly' and in French in *-ment,* e.g.

Il a parlé **lentement**.	*He spoke slowly.*
Elle parle l'anglais **couramment**.	*She speaks English fluently.*

Subject

The **subject** of a verb is the person or thing performing the action or being described. It is the noun or pronoun which governs the verb. e.g.

Jacqueline regarde la carte.

In the above sentence *Jacqueline* is the subject, because it is *Jacqueline* who is looking at the map.

Object

The **object** of a verb is the person or thing which has the action performed on it, e.g.

Il mange **un sandwich**.

In this sentence *un sandwich* is the object, because it is the sandwich which is being eaten.
The object of a sentence can be a noun or a pronoun. If it is a noun it usually comes after the verb, if it is a pronoun it goes between the subject and the verb, e.g.

Il a acheté **des bananes**. On **les** mangera à midi.

Des bananes and *les* ('them') are the objects of the above sentences. They are also examples of the direct object of a sentence.
You may also come across examples of the indirect object. In French, the indirect object (if it is a noun) usually has *à, au* or *aux* in front of it, and in English you can usually put 'to' in front of it, e.g.

J'ai déjà écrit à **mes amis**, mais,	*I have already written to my friends, but*
je **leur** parlerai ce soir au téléphone.	*I will speak to them this evening on the phone.*

Mes amis ('my friends') and *leur* ('them') are the indirect objects of the above sentences.

Prepositions

Prepositions are words like 'to', 'at' *(à)* 'from' *(de)* 'in' *(dans)*, which come before nouns or pronouns and often indicate position, e.g.

In front of her ...	**Devant** elle ...
... at the swimming pool.	... à la piscine.

Negative

A sentence is **negative** when it describes something that is *not, never* or *no longer* happening. 'No-one', 'nothing', 'nowhere' and 'none' are also negatives.

Vowels

The letters **a, e, i, o, u** are vowels in both English and French, and the letter **y** is also a vowel in French. (The other letters of the alphabet are called consonants). Certain words are shortened before a vowel, e.g.

je	→	j'	*as in:* **J**'irai en France un jour.
ne	→	n'	*as in:* Je **n**'ai rien vu.
le	→	l'	*as in:* **l**'oncle Jules
de	→	d'	*as in:* Il n'y a pas **d**'eau.

The letter **h** is often written but not sounded at the beginning of a word. When the h is silent in this way, the above words are also shortened, e.g.

J'hésitais.
L'hôtel de ville.

2 Nouns and articles

2.1 Nouns: masculine and feminine

All nouns in French are either **masculine** or **feminine**:

masculine singular	*feminine singular*
un appartement **le** village **l'**hôtel	**une** maison **la** ville **l'**épicerie

Nouns which describe people or animals often have a special feminine form. Most follow one of the patterns shown in the table opposite.

	masculine singular	feminine singular
1. For the feminine form you add an -**e**	un ami un Français un client un employé de bureau	une ami**e** une Français**e** une client**e** une employé**e** de bureau
2. If the masculine form ends in -**er**, you change this to -**ère**	un ouvrier un infirmier	une ouvri**ère** une infirmi**ère**
3. a) Many masculine nouns which end in -**eur**, have a feminine form ending in -**euse**	un coiffeur un vendeur	une coiff**euse** une vend**euse**
b) However, a few have a feminine form ending in -**rice**	un moniteur de ski un instituteur	une moni**trice** de ski une institu**trice**
4. To convert some masculine nouns, you double the last letter and add an -**e**. (This is common with nouns which end in -**n**)	un lycéen un Parisien un chien un lion un chat	une lycée**nne** une Parisie**nne** une chie**nne** une lio**nne** une cha**tte**
5. The feminine form of some nouns is similar to the English.	un prince un tigre un duc	une princ**esse** une tig**resse** une duch**esse**
6. The feminine forms of some masculine nouns don't follow any clear pattern. You just have to try and remember them separately.	un copain un roi	une copine une reine
7. Remember, not all nouns referring to people have different masculine and feminine forms.	un touriste un élève un enfant	une touriste une élève une enfant

2.2 | Nouns: singular and plural

Nouns can also be **singular** (referring to just one thing or person) or **plural** (referring to more than one thing), e.g.

une chambre   **des** chambres

In many cases, it is easy to use and recognise plural nouns because the last letter is an -**s**. (Remember that this is not usually sounded in spoken French):

un ami ⟶ des ami**s**   un ouvrier ⟶ des ouvrier**s**

Again, there are a few exceptions:

	singular	plural
1. Nouns which end in -**eau** or -**eu** in the singular, add an -**x** for the plural	un château un bateau un jeu	des château**x** des bateau**x** des jeu**x**
2. a) Most nouns which end in -**ou** add an -**s**	un trou	des trou**s**
b) But note these common exceptions	un bijou un chou le genou	des bijou**x** des chou**x** les genou**x**
3. Most nouns which end in -**al**, change this to -**aux**	un animal un journal	des anim**aux** des journ**aux**
4. Nouns which already end in -**s**, -**x**, or -**z** don't change in the plural	un repas le prix	des repas les prix
5. A few nouns don't follow any clear pattern	un œil	des yeux
6. Compound nouns	un porte-monnaie un haut-parleur *BUT* un chou-fleur	des porte-monnaie des haut-parleur**s** des chou**x**-fleur**s**
7. Mr, Mrs and Miss	Monsieur Madame Mademoiselle	Messieurs Mesdames Mesdemoiselles

Note: Surnames in French do not change in the plural:
les Duval   la famille Leclerc *etc.*

| **Collective nouns**

i) **Collective nouns** are considered as singular in French and take the singular form of the verb:

la classe	*the class*	le groupe	*the group*
l'équipe	*the team*	la police	*the police*
la famille	*the family*	le public	*general public*

L'équipe est logée à l'hôtel de Paris.

ii) **Beaucoup, combien** and **la plupart** normally take the plural form of the verb:

Beaucoup (de personnes) ont regardé le match.   *Many (people) watched the match.*

La plupart l'ont suivi attentivement.   *Most (i.e. many of them) followed it attentively.*

2.4 | *le, la, l', les*

The word for 'the' in French is masculine, feminine, singular or plural according to the noun which follows:

masculine singular	*feminine singular*	*before a vowel*	*plural*
le village	**la** ville	**l'**épicerie	**les** touristes

The main uses are as follows:

— to refer to a particular thing or person, in the same way as we use 'the' in English:

C'est **le** village où il y a un bon petit restaurant.   *It's the village where there's a nice little restaurant.*

Voici **l'**hôtel où nous sommes descendus l'année dernière.   *There's the hotel where we stayed last year.*

— to make general statements about likes and dislikes:

J'aime beaucoup **les** frites.

Je n'aime pas **les** carottes.

— and about things as a whole, e.g. *all* dogs, *all* mushrooms:

Les chiens me font toujours peur.

Les champignons me rendent malade.

— with titles:

le Président de la République Française   la reine Elisabeth
la princesse de Galles   Monsieur le Directeur *(the headmaster)*

— with parts of the body:

Il s'est brossé **les** dents.	*He cleaned his teeth.*
J'ai mal à **la** tête.	*I've got a headache.*
Elle a **les** cheveux frisés.	*She's got curly hair.*
Il a ouvert **les** yeux.	*He opened his eyes.*

— with days of the week to give the idea of 'every':

Je vais chez mes grands-parents **le** dimanche.   *(... on Sundays)*

— with different times of the day to mean 'in' or 'during':

Le matin, j'ai cours de 9 heures jusqu'à midi et demi.	*In the morning, I have lessons from 9 o'clock until 12.30.*

— with prices, to refer to a specific quantity:

C'est 5 francs **la** pièce.   C'est 12 francs **le** paquet.

2.5 | *un, une, des*

The word for 'a' or 'an' is masculine or feminine according to the noun which follows:

masculine singular	*feminine singular*	*plural*
un appartement	**une** maison	**des** appartements **des** maisons

It's used when you aren't referring to a specific item, in the same way as we use 'a' or 'an' in English:

Passe-moi **une** cuillère, s'il te plaît.	*Pass me a spoon please.*
Je cherche **un** hôtel, pas trop cher.	*I'm looking for a reasonably-priced hotel.*

Notice that it is omitted when you describe what someone does for a living. In this case, the word for 'a' or 'an' is not translated:

Elle est vendeuse.	*She's a sales assistant.*
Il est employé de bureau.	*He's an office-worker.*

But it is used after *C'est:*

Voilà son père. C'est **un** médecin.   *He's a doctor.*
Voilà sa sœur. C'est **une** technicienne.   *She's a technician.*

2.6   *du, de la, de l', des*

The word for 'some' or 'any' agrees with the noun which follows:

masculine singular	feminine singular	before a vowel	plural
du pain	**de la** viande	**de l'**eau **de l'**huile	**des** pommes

It's used to mean 'some' or 'any' or to refer to a substance (such as sugar, water, milk) which you can't count:

Avez-vous **du** pain?   *Have you any bread?*
Voulez-vous encore **de la** viande?   *Would you like some more meat?*
C'est **de l'**eau potable?   *Is it drinking water?*
Elle a acheté **des** pommes.   *She bought some apples.*
Vous prenez **du** lait et **du** sucre?   *Do you take milk and sugar?*

2.7   *de*

Notice that **de** is used instead of *du, de la, de l'* and *des* and *un* and *une* in the following situations:

— after a negative, such as 'not', 'no more', 'never' etc.:

Je suis désolé, mais je n'ai plus **de** pain.
Je regrette, il ne reste plus **de** place.
On ne vend pas **de** pellicules dans une pharmacie en France.
J'ai une sœur, mais je n'ai pas **de** frères.

Note: This does not happen with the verb *être* or after *ne ... que,* e.g.

Ce n'est pas du sucre, c'est du sel.
Je n'ai qu'un billet.   *I've only got one ticket.*

— after many expressions of quantity:

Il y a beaucoup **d'**Anglais au camping.
Un peu **de** fromage, s'il vous plaît.
Un paquet **de** biscuits, un kilo **de** poires, une boîte **de** sardines et une bouteille **de** limonade, s'il vous plaît.
100 grammes **de** pâté et une portion **de** salade de tomates, s'il vous plaît.
On aurait dû acheter plus **de** vin.   *We should have bought more wine.*

— usually when an adjective comes before the noun:

Ce sont **de** bons amis.
Elle est **de** mauvaise humeur.

See also: 4.4   **de** + noun
                13.2   **de** as a preposition

3   'This', 'that', 'these', 'those'

3.1   *ce, cet, cette, ces*

The different forms of **ce** are used when you want to point out a particular thing or person:

masculine singular		feminine singular		plural
	before a vowel		*before a vowel*	
ce chapeau	**cet** anorak	**cette** jupe	**cette** écharpe	**ces** chaussures

Ce can mean either 'this' or 'that'. **Ces** can mean either 'these' or 'those'. If you want to be more precise, you can add **-ci** to the noun for 'this', and **-là** for 'that':

Est-ce que tu préfères **ce** pull-**ci** ou **ce** pull-**là**?
Je vais acheter **cette** robe-**là**.

Do you prefer this pullover or that pullover?
I'm going to buy that dress.

3.2 celui, celle, ceux, celles

When 'this' or 'that' is not followed by a noun, use **celui, celle, ceux** or **celles**. To distinguish between 'this one' and 'that one' add -ci or -là:

masculine singular	feminine singular	masculine plural	feminine plural
celui-ci *this one* **celui-là** *that one*	**celle-ci** *this one* **celle-là** *that one*	**ceux-ci** *these* **ceux-là** *those*	**celles-ci** *these* **celles-là** *those*

Nous avons deux appartements à louer.   *We have two flats to rent.*
Celui-ci se trouve au centre-ville.   *This one ...*
Celui-là se trouve dans la banlieue.   *That one ...*

Celui, celle, ceux and **celles** can also be used in a sentence to save repeating a noun and to give the meaning of 'the one' or 'the ones':

— Tu reconnais ce disque?
— Oui, c'est **celui** que nous avons écouté chez Marc, n'est-ce pas?
— C'est ta voiture, ça?
— Non, c'est **celle** de mon père.
— Ce sont tes nouvelles chaussures?
— Oui, ce sont **celles** que j'ai achetées ce matin.

3.3 ça, ceci and cela

If there is no noun or you want to refer to a general idea, the pronouns **ceci** meaning 'this' and **cela** (or **ça**) meaning 'that' can be used:

Ça, c'est une bonne idée.   *That's a good idea.*
Cela n'a pas d'importance.   *That's not important.*
Aïe! **Ça** me fait mal!   *Ouch! That hurts.*
Ce qui nous concerne est **ceci**:   *The thing that concerns us is this:*

4 Expressing possession

4.1 | *mon, ma, mes* etc.

These possessive adjectives go with nouns to show *who* something or someone belongs to. They agree with the noun which follows (not with the person who owns the thing):

	masculine singular	feminine singular	before a vowel	plural
my *your* *his, her, its* *our* *your* *their*	**mon** **ton** **son** **notre** **votre** **leur**	**ma** **ta** **sa** **notre** **votre** **leur**	**mon** **ton** **son** **notre** **votre** **leur**	**mes** **tes** **ses** **nos** **vos** **leurs**

Notice that **son, sa, ses** can mean 'his', 'her' or 'its'. The meaning is usually clear from the context:

Paul mange **sa** viande.   *Paul eats his meat.*

Marie mange **sa** viande.   *Marie eats her meat.*

Le chien mange **sa** viande.   *The dog eats its meat.*

Before a feminine noun beginning with a vowel, you use **mon, ton** or **son**:

Mon affiche préférée est celle d'Air France.

Où habite **ton** amie, Françoise?

Son école est fermée aujourd'hui.

Note:

1. You should not use possessive adjectives with parts of the body. *(See 4:5).*
2. When using more than one noun, you must repeat the possessive adjective, e.g.

Ses frères et **ses** sœurs.   *His brothers and sisters.*

4.2 | *le mien, le tien* etc.

	masculine singular	*feminine singular*	*masculine plural*	*feminine plural*
mine	le mien	la mienne	les miens	les miennes
yours	le tien	la tienne	les tiens	les tiennes
his, hers, its	le sien	la sienne	les siens	les siennes
ours	le nôtre	la nôtre	les nôtres	les nôtres
yours	le vôtre	la vôtre	les vôtres	les vôtres
theirs	le leur	la leur	les leurs	les leurs

You use these possessive pronouns when the noun is not repeated. Again, there are
different forms for masculine, feminine, singular and plural:

- C'est ton sac, là?
- Non, c'est celui de Monique. **Le mien** est là-bas. *Mine is over there.*
- Leur appartement est plus grand que **le nôtre.** *Their flat is bigger than ours.*

4.3 | *à moi, à toi* etc.

mine	à moi	*ours*	à nous
yours	à toi	*yours*	à vous
his	à lui	*theirs*	à eux
hers	à elle	*theirs*	à elles

In conversational French, it is more common to use the above to say 'mine', 'yours' and
so on than it is to say *le mien, le tien* etc.:

- C'est à qui, ce stylo?
- C'est **à moi**.
- Les cartes postales sont **à toi**, aussi?

4.4 | *de* + noun

There is no use of apostrophe 's' in French, so to translate 'Marie-Claire's house' or 'Olivier's skis', you have to use **de** followed by the name of the owner:

C'est la maison **de** Marie-Claire.
Ce sont les skis **d'**Olivier.

If you don't actually name the person, you have to use the appropriate form of **de** (**du, de la, de l'** or **des**):

— C'est la tente **de la** famille anglaise.
— C'est votre journal?
— Non, c'est celui **du** monsieur qui vient de sortir.

4.5 | *le, la, l', les* + parts of the body

In French, the definite article (**le, la, l', les**) is normally used with parts of the body:

Elle s'est lavé **les** mains.	*She washed her hands.*
Il s'est coupé **le** doigt.	*He cut his finger.*

5   Asking questions

5.1 | Using your voice

In conversational French, you will find that people change a simple statement into a question simply by raising their voice in a questioning way:

Tu viens?	*Are you coming?*
Vous sortez?	*Are you going out?*

5.2 | Using *Est-ce que ...*

You can make any statement into a question by adding **Est-ce que** to the beginning of the sentence:

Est-ce que vous restez longtemps en France?	*Are you staying in France for long?*
Est-ce qu'il reste du café?	*Is there any coffee left?*

5.3 | Using *n'est-ce pas?*

N'est-ce pas is used when you are expecting someone to agree with you. Roughly translated it means 'don't you think?' or 'isn't it?':

Il fait froid, **n'est-ce pas?**   *It's cold, isn't it?*

5.4 | Using inversion

A more formal way of asking questions, particularly found in written French, is to turn round (invert) the verb and the subject:

Jouez-vous au badminton?   *Do you play badminton?*

Notice that if the verb ends in a vowel in the 3rd person, you have to add an extra **-t** when you turn it round:

Joue-t-il au football?   *Does he play football?*

Marie, **a-t-elle** ton adresse?   *Has Marie got your address?*

In the Perfect Tense, you just turn the auxiliary verb and the subject round:

Avez-vous vu le film au cinéma Rex?

As-tu écrit à Paul?

Jean et Pierre, **sont-ils** allés au match hier?

Monique, **a-t-elle** téléphoné à Chantal?

Note: Inversion is rarely used with the *je* form.

5.5 | Standard answers

Oui.	*Yes.*
Si.	*Yes* (with emphasis or in contradiction to what someone has just said)
Je crois que oui.	*I think so.*
Volontiers.	*Willingly.*
Avec plaisir.	*With pleasure.*
Bien sûr.	*Of course.*
Je veux bien.	*I'd really like to.*
Non.	*No.*
Je crois que non.	*I don't think so.*
Pas du tout.	*Not at all.*
Absolument pas!	*Certainly not!*

Question forms

À quelle heure?	*At what time?*
De quelle couleur?	*What colour?*
Combien?	*How much? How many?*
Comment?	*How?*
Comment est-il?	*What's he like?*
Où?	*Where?*
D'où vient-il?	*Where's he from?*
Pourquoi?	*Why?*
Quand?	*When?*
Que...?	*What?*
Qu'est-ce que c'est?	*What is it?*
Qu'est-ce qu'il y a?	*What's the matter?*
Qu'est-ce qui ne va pas?	*What's wrong?*
Qui?	*Who?*
Qui est-ce?	*Who is it?*
Avec qui?	*With whom?*
Quoi?	*What?*
De quoi s'agit-il?	*What's it all about?*

5.7 | 'Who' and 'whom?'

If 'who' is the subject of the verb, use **qui** or **qui est-ce qui**:

Qui vient ce soir?	*Who's coming this evening?*
Qui est-ce qui le dit?	*Who says so?*

If 'who' ('whom') is the object of the verb, you can still use **qui** but you must turn the verb and the subject round:

Qui voyez-vous à l'hôpital?	*Who (whom) are you seeing at the hospital?*

Alternatively you can use **Qui est-ce que**:

Qui est-ce que vous cherchez?	*Who (whom) are you looking for?*

Qui is used with prepositions to say 'with whom', 'for whom', 'about whom' etc.:

Elle sort **avec qui**?	*Who is she going out with?*
Avec qui part-il en vacances?	*Who is he going on holiday with?*

5.8 | 'What?'

If 'what' is the subject of the sentence, use **Qu'est-ce qui**:

Qu'est-ce qui ne va pas?	*What's wrong?*
Qu'est-ce qui s'est passé?	*What's happened?*

If 'what' is the object of the verb, you can either use **que** and turn the verb and the subject round:

Que désirez-vous?	*What do you want?*

or you can use **Qu'est-ce que**:

Qu'est-ce qu'il a dit?	*What did he say?*
Qu'est-ce que tu veux?	*What do you want?*

Quoi is used with prepositions, such as *à, avec, de, en:*

C'est fait en **quoi**?	*What's it made of?*
À **quoi** penses-tu?	*What are you thinking about?*

5.9 | *quel* and *lequel*

masculine singular	feminine singular	masculine plural	feminine plural
quel	quelle	quels	quelles
lequel	laquelle	lesquels	lesquelles

Quel is an adjective and means 'what' or 'which'. Like all adjectives, it agrees with the noun which follows:

Quel est votre nom?	*What is your name?*
Quelle est son adresse?	*What is his address?*
Quels journaux lisez-vous?	*Which newspapers do you read?*
Quelles chaussures vas-tu mettre?	*Which shoes are you going to wear?*

Lequel is a pronoun and means 'which one(s)?' Like all pronouns, it is used instead of repeating a noun:

- Passe-moi le livre.
- **Lequel?**
- Le Guide de Paris.
- Tu peux m'envoyer ces photos?
- **Lesquelles?**
- Celles de nos vacances à Marseille.

6 Adjectives

Adjectives are words which tell you more about a noun. Notice how they are used in the following sentence to give a much clearer description of the monster. All the words underlined are adjectives:

It was a _big_, _green_ animal with four _short_ legs.
C'était un **grand** animal **vert** à quatre **petites** pattes.

6.1 Agreement of adjectives

Adjectives change their form according to the noun they describe. They are then said to 'agree' with that noun. They can be masculine, feminine, singular or plural:

Regular adjectives

	masculine singular	feminine singular	masculine plural	feminine plural
1. Many adjectives follow this pattern.	grand intelligent fort français allemand	grande intelligente forte française allemande	grands intelligents forts français* allemands	grandes intelligentes fortes françaises allemandes
2. Adjectives which end in -u, i or é follow this pattern, but although the spelling changes, they don't sound any different when you say them.	bleu joli fatigué âgé	bleue jolie fatiguée âgée	bleus jolis fatigués âgés	bleues jolies fatiguées âgées

	masculine singular	feminine singular	masculine plural	feminine plural
3. Adjectives which already end in -e (with no accent) have no different feminine form.	jaune mince stupide jeune	jaune mince stupide jeune	jaunes minces stupides jeunes	jaunes minces stupides jeunes
4. Adjectives which end in -er follow this pattern.	cher premier	chère première	chers premiers	chères premières
5. Adjectives which end in -x follow this pattern.	affreux délicieux merveilleux	affreuse délicieuse merveilleuse	affreux* délicieux* merveilleux*	affreuses délicieuses merveilleuses
6. Some adjectives double the last letter before adding an -e for the feminine form.	gentil mignon gros bon	gentille mignonne grosse bonne	gentils mignons gros* bons	gentilles mignonnes grosses bonnes

Irregular adjectives

	masculine singular	feminine singular	masculine plural	feminine plural
Many common adjectives are irregular, and each one has to be learnt separately. Here are some of the most common ones.	beau (bel**) blanc bref doux faux favori fou (fol**) frais long neuf nouveau (nouvel**) sec vieux (vieil**)	belle blanche brève douce fausse favorite folle fraîche longue neuve nouvelle sèche vieille	beaux blancs brefs doux faux favoris fous frais longs neufs nouveaux secs vieux*	belles blanches brèves douces fausses favorites folles fraîches longues neuves nouvelles sèches vieilles

* If the adjective already ends in -s or -x in the masculine singular, it doesn't change in the plural form.

** A few adjectives have a different masculine form which is used when the following word begins with a vowel or a silent *h*.

un **vieil** homme   un **nouvel** élève   un **bel** appareil-photo, un **fol** espoir

6.2 Useful adjectives

noir	black	carré	square-shaped
blanc	white	rond	round
bleu	blue	moderne	modern
vert	green	vieux	old
brun	brown	jeune	young
gris	grey	âgé	old
rouge	red	long	long
jaune	yellow	court	short
clair	light	propre	clean
foncé	dark	sale	dirty
blond	blond	célèbre	famous
marron*	brown	bien connu	well-known
grand	tall, big	triste	sad
petit	small	content	happy
étroit	narrow	beau	good-looking, fine, beautiful
large	wide		
maigre	thin	laid	ugly
mince	slim	joli	pretty
gros	big, fat	bon	good
fort	well-built, strong	mauvais	bad

* **marron** is invariable (it doesn't change form)

6.3 Position of adjectives

i) Adjectives normally follow the noun. This is always the case with adjectives of colour and nationality:

J'ai lu un article très **intéressant** sur le camping en France.

Tu aimes cette jupe **noire?**

Nous avons une voiture **française.**

ii) However, there are a few common, usually short adjectives which go in front of the noun:

beau	gentil	jeune	petit
bon	grand	joli	vieux
court	gros	long	
excellent	haut	mauvais	

C'est un **petit** garçon d'environ six ans.

La Loire est un **long** fleuve.

iii) Some adjectives alter their meaning depending on whether they come before or after the noun. Here are a few of the most common ones:

ancien	un **ancien** élève *a former pupil*
	un bâtiment **ancien** *an old (ancient) building*
cher	un **cher** ami *a dear friend*
	un hôtel **cher** *an expensive hotel*
même	la **même** robe *the same dress*
	le jour **même** *the very day*
	le Président **même** *the President himself*
pauvre	**pauvre** Nicole *poor old Nicole*
	un pays **pauvre** *a poor (not wealthy) country*
propre	Elle a son **propre** appartement. *She's got her own flat.*
	Je n'ai pas de chemise **propre**. *I haven't got a clean shirt.*

6.4 | Adjectives followed by prepositions

Je suis **obligé de** lui téléphoner.
Il est **impossible de** partir.
C'est **impossible à** faire.
Elle est **contente de** le voir.
Tu es **prêt à** partir?
Il est **fort en** maths.

Christine n'est pas très **forte en** histoire.
Regarde ton pantalon. Il est **couvert de** boue. *(covered in mud)*

6.5 | *il est* or *c'est* + adjective

Notice when to use **il est** + an adjective and when to use **c'est**:

— **Il est** difficile d'apprendre le français.
— Mais non. Apprendre le français, **c'est** facile!

If you go on to say at the end of the sentence *what* is difficult (or whatever), then you use **il est**.
If, however, the thing that is difficult (or easy) has already been mentioned or understood, then you use **c'est**.

So you could say that **il est** points forward, and **c'est** refers back. Here are some more examples:

— **Il est** impossible d'aller en France cette année.
— Quel dommage! L'année dernière, **c'était** vraiment formidable.
— **Il est** magnifique, ce chapeau, n'est-ce pas?
— Tu trouves? À mon avis, **c'est** affreux!

6.6 Making comparisons

To compare one person or thing with another, you use **plus** *(more...)*, **moins** *(less ...)*, **aussi** *(as ...)*, **si** *(as ... in a negative sentence)* + adjective + **que:**

Il est **plus** riche **que** mon père, *(richer)*
mais il est **moins** intelligent. *(less intelligent)*
Elle est **aussi** célèbre **que** sa mère, *(as famous)*
mais elle n'est pas **si** belle. *(not as beautiful)*

Remember to make the adjective agree in the usual way:

Ce restaurant est plus **cher** que l'autre.
Cette robe est plus **chère** que l'autre.
Ces skis sont plus **chers** que les autres.
Ces chaussures sont plus **chères** que les autres.

Notice these special forms:

bon   ⟶   **meilleur, meilleure, meilleurs, meilleures** *(better)*
mauvais ⟶   **pire, pires** *(worse)*
                  (or: **plus mauvais (mauvaise, mauvais, mauvaises)**

Ce café est **meilleur** que l'autre. *(better)*
Ce vin est mauvais, mais l'autre est encore **pire.** *(even worse)*

6.7 Superlative

To say that something is 'the best', 'the greatest', 'the fastest', 'the biggest', 'the most expensive' etc., you use a **superlative.** This is formed like the comparative but with *le, la* or *les* in front:

La Tour Eiffel est **le plus haut** monument de Paris.	*The Eiffel Tower is the highest monument in Paris.*
Paris est **la plus belle** ville du monde.	*Paris is the most beautiful city in the world.*
Les TGV sont les trains français **les plus rapides.**	*The TGV are the fastest French trains.*

Notice that:

— you use **le, la, les** and the correct form of the adjective, depending on whether you are describing something which is masculine, feminine, singular or plural.

— if the adjective normally goes after the noun, then the superlative also follows the noun:

C'est le monument **le plus moderne** de Paris.

— if the adjective normally goes before the noun, then the superlative also goes before the noun:

C'est **le plus haut** monument de Paris.

— you usually use **plus** (meaning 'most') but you can also use **moins** (meaning 'least').

— you use **de (du, de la, de l')** after the superlative, to mean 'in' or 'of':

J'ai choisi cet hôtel, parce que   *I chose this hotel, because it was the*
c'était le moins cher **de** tous.   *least expensive (cheapest) of them all.*

Useful expressions:

le moins cher	*the least expensive*
le plus cher	*the most expensive*
le plus petit	*the smallest*
le plus grand	*the biggest*
le meilleur	*the best*
le pire	*the worst*

7 Adverbs

Adverbs are words which add extra meaning to the verb. They usually tell you *how, when* or *where* something happened or *how much* something is done. Many adverbs in English end in '-ly' e.g. 'badly', 'frequently', 'quietly'.

7.1 Formation of adverbs

Most adverbs in French end in **-ment**.

i) This is usually added to the feminine form of the adjective:

masculine singular	feminine singular	adverb	meaning
général	générale	**généralement**	usually
doux	douce	**doucement**	quietly
malheureux	malheureuse	**malheureusement**	unfortunately
Exception: gentil	gentille	**gentiment**	kindly

ii) If the adjective ends in a vowel in the masculine singular, add **-ment** directly to this:

masculine singular	adverb	meaning
vrai	**vraiment**	really
rare	**rarement**	rarely
facile	**facilement**	easily

iii) If the adjective ends in -ent or -ant in the masculine singular, the adverb follows this pattern:

masculine singular	adverb	meaning
récent	**récemment**	recently
patient	**patiemment**	patiently
évident	**évidemment**	obviously
fréquent	**fréquemment**	frequently
Exception:		
lent	**lentement**	slowly

iv) In some cases the final **e** of the feminine form of the adjective becomes **é**:

masculine singular	feminine singular	adverb	meaning
énorme précis	énorme précise	**énormément précisément**	hugely exactly

v) Not all adverbs end in -**ment**. There are quite a lot of useful adverbs which have different endings. Here are some of the most common:

beaucoup	*a lot*	**peu**	*not much*
bien	*well*	**tard**	*late*
loin	*far*	**tôt**	*early*
longtemps	*for a long time*	**vite**	*quickly*
mal	*badly*		

vi) A few adjectives can be used as adverbs without changing their form:

bon	Ça sent **bon**.	*That smells nice.*
bas	Ils parlaient **bas**.	*They were speaking quietly.*
cher	Ça coûte trop **cher**.	*That costs too much.*
faux	Elle chante **faux**.	*She's singing out of tune.*
fort	Tu peux parler plus **fort**?	*Can you speak more loudly?*

7.2 | Position of the adverb

In most cases, the adverb goes after the verb:

Tu comprends **parfaitement**.
Elle marche très **lentement**.

With the Perfect Tense and the Pluperfect Tense, however, the adverb usually goes between the auxiliary verb and the past participle, unless the adverb is a particularly long one:

Avez-vous **bien** dormi?
Elle ne m'a **même** pas écrit.
Il a conduit **dangereusement**.
Elle a parlé **continuellement**.

7.3 | Comparative and superlative

As with adjectives, you can use adverbs to make comparisons by adding **plus** ('more'), **moins** ('less'), **aussi** ('as'), **si** ('as' with a negative) before the adverb:

— Elle conduit **plus vite** que son mari.
— Mais elle ne conduit pas **si vite** que sa fille.
L'année dernière, Simone jouait **très bien** au tennis, mais cette année, elle joue **moins bien**.
— Marc joue bien au football, n'est-ce pas?
— Oui, il joue **aussi bien** que son frère.

Adverbs can also be used as superlatives by adding **le plus** or **le moins** in front of the adverb:

Je viendrai **le plus vite** possible.
Il ne comprend pas le français. Parlez **le moins vite** possible.

The following adverbs, which have rather special forms, are frequently used in French:

adverb		comparative		superlative	
bien	well	mieux	better	le mieux	the best
beaucoup	a lot	plus	more	le plus	the most
peu	not much	moins	less	le moins	the least
mal	badly	pire	worse	le pire	the worst

Ça va **mieux** aujourd'hui?
N'achète pas cette robe; c'est celle que j'aime **le moins**.
C'est lui, qui travaille **le plus**.

Are you feeling better today?
Don't buy that dress; it's the one I like the least.
He works the hardest.

Notice that you can use **surtout** to mean 'most' or 'above all':

Qu'est-ce que tu as **surtout** aimé à Paris?   *What did you like most in Paris?*

7.4 | Intensifiers and qualifiers

The following words can be used with adverbs or adjectives to add extra meaning:

assez	*quite, enough*
beaucoup	*much*
de moins en moins	*less and less*
de plus en plus	*more and more*
presque	*almost*
tant	*so much, too*
tellement	*so (much)*
tout à fait	*completely, quite*
très	*very*
trop	*too*

La voiture bleue ne roule pas **assez** vite.	*The blue car isn't going fast enough.*
Il court beaucoup **trop** lentement.	*He is running much too slowly.*
Il est **tout à fait** capable de le faire.	*He's quite capable of doing it.*
Elle parle le français **presque** aussi bien qu'une Française.	*She speaks French almost as well as a French person.*
Tant mieux.	*So much the better.*
Tant pis.	*Too bad.*
Il a conduit **de plus en plus** vite.	*He drove faster and faster.*
Elle y va **de moins en moins** souvent.	*She goes there less and less often.*

8 | Negatives

8.1 | 'Never', 'not', 'nothing', 'no more' etc.

Negative expressions in French usually consist of two parts. These are the most common ones:

ne ... pas	*not*
ne ... plus	*no more, no longer, none left*
ne ... jamais	*never*
ne ... rien	*nothing*
ne ... personne	*nobody*
ne ... que	*only*
ne ... nulle part	*nowhere, not ... anywhere*
ne ... aucun	*no (see 8.5)*
ne ... ni ... ni	*neither ... nor, not ... either ... or*

8.2 | Position

As a general rule, the negative goes on either side of the verb:

Je n'aime **pas** ça.	*I don't like that.*
Elles **ne** vont **plus** au lycée.	*They no longer go to school.*
On **ne** sort **jamais**.	*We never go out.*
Il **n'**y a **rien** à la télé.	*There's nothing on TV.*
Elle **ne** connaît **personne** à Paris.	*She doesn't know anyone in Paris.*
Je **n'**ai **que** dix francs sur moi.	*I have only 10 francs on me.*
Je **ne** le vois **nulle part**.	*I can't see him anywhere.*
Je **n'**en ai **aucune** idée.	*I have no idea.*
Il **n'**a **ni** amis **ni** argent.	*He has neither friends nor money.*

If there is a pronoun before the verb, the **ne** goes before that:

Il **ne** se lève pas tôt.	*He doesn't get up early.*
Ne le mange pas!	*Don't eat it!*

Before an infinitive, the two parts of the negative come together:

Je l'ai persuadé de **ne pas** partir.	*I persuaded him not to leave.*
Elle m'a promis de **ne plus** le voir.	*She promised me that she wouldn't see him anymore.*

8.3 | Perfect and Pluperfect Tenses in the negative

Most negatives go round the auxiliary verb:

Je **n'**ai **pas** compris.	*I don't understand.*
Il **n'**a **plus** voulu travailler à Paris.	*He didn't want to work in Paris any longer.*
Elle **n'**est **jamais** allée aux États-Unis.	*She has never been to the USA.*
Tu **n'**as **rien** fait ce matin?	*Didn't you do anything this morning?*

However, with the following negatives, the second part normally goes after the past participle:

ne ... personne
ne ... que
ne ... nulle part

On **n'**a vu **personne** en ville.	*We didn't see anyone in town.*
Je **n'**ai passé **qu'**un après-midi à Marseille.	*I only spent an afternoon at Marseille.*
Elle a cherché partout son porte-monnaie, mais elle **ne** l'a trouvé **nulle part**.	*She's looked everywhere for her purse, but she hasn't found it anywhere.*

With **ne ... ni ... ni**, put **ni ... ni ...** where you would say 'neither ... nor' in English:

Pendant son séjour à Paris, il **n'**a visité *During his stay in Paris, he visited neither*
ni le Centre Pompidou **ni** le Forum. *the Pompidou Centre nor the Forum.*

Il **ne** savait **ni** lire **ni** écrire. *He could neither read nor write.*

8.4 | *rien, jamais* and *personne*

Notice that **rien, jamais** and **personne** can also be used on their own:

- — Qu'est-ce que tu as fait, ce matin?
- — **Rien** de spécial.
- — Qui est dans le garage?
- — **Personne.**
- — Avez-vous déjà fait du ski?
- — Non, **jamais.**

Rien and **personne** can also be used at the beginning of the sentence, as the subject of the verb:

Rien n'est plus facile. *Nothing is easier.*
Personne n'est venu. *Nobody came.*

8.5 | *ne ... aucun* ('no', 'not one')

Ne ... aucun is used quite a lot in conversational French. **Aucun** is an adjective, so, like other adjectives, it agrees with the noun which follows:

Il **n'**y a **aucun** doute. *There's no doubt.* (masculine singular)
Ça **n'a aucune** importance. *That is of no importance.* (feminine singular)

8.6 | After the negative

After the negative, **du, de la, de l', des, un** and **une** become **de** or **d'** (except with the verb *être* and after *ne ... que*):

On ne vend pas **de** lait. *They don't sell milk.*
Il ne reste plus **de** pain. *There's no bread left.*
Je n'ai pas **de** frères. *I haven't any brothers.*
Tu n'as jamais mangé **d'**escargots? *Have you never eaten snails?*

If you want to contradict someone or re-affirm something, you use **si** instead of *oui:*

- — Vous n'avez jamais visité Notre-Dame, n'est-ce pas?
- — Mais **si**. J'y suis allé l'année dernière.

8.7 | *ne* on its own; *pas* on its own

Notice that **ne (n')** is used on its own in the following expressions:

N'importe quoi.	*No matter what; Anything.*
N'importe qui.	*No matter who; Anyone.*
Un certain je **ne** sais quoi.	*A certain something.*

When there is no verb, **pas** can be used on its own:

pas encore	*not yet*
pas tout à fait	*not quite*
pas du tout	*not at all*

Occasionally, **non** is used in the middle of a sentence:

C'est pour ton frère et **non** pas pour toi.

8.8 | Useful expressions

Je n'ai pas le temps.	*I haven't time.*
Il n'y a pas de raison.	*There's no need to.*
Il n'en est pas question.	*There's no question of it.*
Ne vous inquiétez pas.	*Don't worry.*
Je n'en veux plus.	*I don't want any more.*
N'en parlons plus.	*Don't let's talk about it any more.*
On ne sait jamais!	*You never know.*
Jamais de la vie!	*Not on your life; Over my dead body.*
Rien de plus facile.	*Nothing easier.*
Ça ne fait rien.	*It doesn't matter.*
Il n'y a rien à faire.	*Nothing can be done.*
Je n'y peux rien.	*I can't do anything about it.*
Il n'y a personne.	*There's no-one there.*
Il ne reste que ça.	*That's all there is left.*
Ni l'un ni l'autre.	*Neither of them.*
Ni moi non plus.	*Nor me.*

Notice that two or more negatives can be used together:

Rien ne va **plus**.	*No more bets* (used in roulette, lit. *Nothing goes any more)*
Personne ne fait **plus jamais rien**.	*Nobody ever does anything any more.*
La bibliothèque **n'**est **plus** ouverte **que** le jeudi.	*The library is now only open on Thursdays.*

9 Pronouns (subject and object)

9.1 Subject pronouns

Subject pronouns are words like 'I', 'you', 'he', 'she', 'it' etc. They are used to replace a noun which is the subject of the sentence.

je (or **j'**)	*I*	**nous**	*we*
tu	*you*	**vous**	*you* (plural or formal)
il	*he* (or *it*)	**ils**	*they*
elle	*she* (or *it*)	**elles**	*they*
on	*one, we, people in general*		

tu or *vous*

When speaking to strangers, officials or people older than yourself, you should normally use **vous**. Tu is used when speaking to close friends or relatives, children, animals and often to colleagues of a similar age. It can be difficult to know when it is appropriate to call an adult **tu** so it is best to let the French person decide this. It implies greater familiarity than calling someone by their Christian name.

On peut se tutoyer?
On peut se dire 'tu'? } *Shall we call each other* tu?

il/elle ils/elles

Notice that **il** can mean 'he' or 'it' (when referring to things or animals that are masculine). Similarly, **elle** can mean 'she' or 'it' (when referring to things or animals which are feminine). With the plural forms, **ils** is used for a group of men or boys or a mixed group, whereas **elles** is only used with a group of women or girls.

on

On is a very useful little word which is used a great deal in conversational French. Its exact meaning is often vague; it can mean 'someone', 'people in general', 'we', 'they', 'you' and 'one':

Si **on** allait au cinéma?	*Shall we go to the cinema?*
On parle français en Tunisie.	*People speak French in Tunisia.*
On m'a dit de venir vous voir.	*Someone told me to come and see you.*
On peut acheter des timbres au bureau de tabac.	*You (one) can buy stamps at a tobacconist's.*

9.2 | *le, la, l', les* (direct object pronouns)

These pronouns replace a noun, or a phrase containing a noun, which is not the subject of the verb. They can refer to people or things and are frequently used as they save having to repeat a noun or phrase.

Le is used instead of a masculine singular noun:

- Tu connais Pierre Duval?
- Oui, je **le** connais très bien.

La is used instead of a feminine singular noun:

- Vous prenez la jupe?
- Non, je ne **la** prends pas, elle est trop petite.

L' is used when the next word in the sentence begins with a vowel:

- Tu as lu le journal, ce matin?
- Oui, je **l'**ai lu dans le train.

Les is used instead of a plural noun:

- Tu as acheté des billets pour le train?
- Non, pas encore. Je **les** achèterai ce soir.

Notice that the pronoun usually goes before the verb, even when the verb is a question or in the negative:

- Tu **le** vois?
- Non, je ne **le** vois pas.

This also happens when the pronoun is used with an infinitive:

Quand est-ce que vous allez **les** voir?

In the Perfect Tense, the object pronoun goes before the auxiliary verb *(See also* 9.5):

C'est un bon film. Tu **l'**as vu?

However, with commands, the pronoun goes after the verb:

- Où est-ce qu'on met la table et les chaises?
- Mettez-**les** dans la salle à manger.

except when the command is in the negative:

Ne **les** mettez pas dans la cuisine.

These pronouns can also be used with *voici* and *voilà:*

- Vous avez votre billet?
- **Le voilà.**

— Tu as ta carte?
— **La voilà.**
— Où sont Philippe et Monique?
— **Les voilà.**

9.3 | *lui* and *leur* (indirect object pronouns)

Lui is used to replace masculine or feminine singular nouns, often in a phrase beginning with *à*. It usually means 'to *or* for him' or 'to *or* for her':

— Qu'est-ce que tu vas offrir à ta sœur?
— Je vais **lui** offrir un disque.
— Et à ton frère?
— Je vais **lui** offrir un livre.

In the same way, **leur** is used to replace masculine or feminine plural nouns, often in a phrase beginning with *à* or *aux:*

— Tu as déjà téléphoné à tes parents?
— Non, mais je vais **leur** téléphoner, ce soir.

9.4 | *me, te, nous, vous*

These pronouns are used as both direct and indirect object pronouns.

Me (or **m'**) means 'me', 'to *or* for me':

Zut! elle **m'**a vu.
— Est-ce que tu peux **m'**acheter un timbre?
— Oui, si tu **me** donnes de l'argent.

Te (or **t'**) means 'you', 'to *or* for you':

Henri ..., Henri, je **te** parles. Qui **t'**a donné cet argent?

Nous means 'us', 'to *or* for us':

Jean-Pierre vient **nous** chercher à la maison.
Il **nous** écrit souvent.

Vous means 'you', 'to *or* for you':

On **vous** attend au café.
Je **vous** rendrai les disques, la semaine prochaine.

9.5 | Direct object pronouns in the Perfect Tense

When **le, la, l'** or **les** are used in the Perfect Tense, with verbs which take *avoir,* the past participle agrees with the pronoun:

- Où as-tu acheté ton pull?
- Je l'ai acheté à Paris.   (masculine singular)
- Tu as vu Chantal en ville?
- Oui, je l'ai vue au supermarché.   (feminine singular)
- Tu as déjà écouté tes nouveaux disques?
- Oui, je **les** ai écoutés dans le magasin. (masculine plural)
- As-tu acheté tes chaussures de ski?
- Non, je **les** ai louées. (feminine plural)

The same rule applies to **me, te, nous, vous** when they are used as direct object pronouns, i.e. when they mean 'me', 'you', 'us', 'you':

Vous **nous** avez **vus** au concert?   *Did you see us at the concert?*

9.6 | Emphatic or 'strong' pronouns

The pronouns described so far can only be used with a verb. **Emphatic** or **'strong' pronouns** are sometimes used with a verb, but can also be used on their own:

moi	*me*	nous	*us*
toi	*you*	vous	*you*
lui	*him*	eux	*them*
elle	*her*	elles	*them*
soi	*oneself*		

The main uses are:

— for emphasis:

Moi, je vais toujours en France pendant les vacances, mais **lui,** il préfère aller en Espagne.

— after *c'est* or *ce sont:*

- Qui est-ce?
- C'est **nous.**   *It's us.*

Ce sont **eux.**   *It's them.*

— on their own or after *pas:*

    — Qui est là?
    — **Moi.**   *Me.*
    — Qui a fait ça?
    — Pas **moi.**   *Not me.*

— after prepositions, such as 'with', 'without', 'for', 'before', 'after,' 'in front of', 'behind' etc.:

... devant **moi.**	*... in front of me.*
Il est parti avant **elle.**	*... before her.*
... après **vous.**	*... after you.*
Faites comme chez **vous.**	*Make yourself at home.*

— in comparisons:

    Je suis plus riche que **toi.**
    Elle joue mieux que **lui.**

— with **même** to mean '-self':

Je l'ai fait **moi-même.**	*... myself.*
Nous avons construit la maison **nous-mêmes.**	*... ourselves.*

Note: Soi means 'oneself' or 'himself', but should only be used with *on, chacun, personne, tout le monde* or after *chez:*

Chacun pour **soi.**	*Each for himself.*
On est bien chez **soi.**	*It's good to be in your own home.*

— after *à* to show who something belongs to:

    Ce disque est à **moi,** l'autre est à **lui.**

9.7   Order of pronouns

Occasionally two pronouns are used together in a sentence. When this happens, the following rule applies:

me te nous vous	come before	le la les	come before	lui leur

Qui **te l'**a dit?	*Who told you that?*
Je **le lui** ai souvent dit.	*I've often told him so.*
Elle **me l'**a donné.	*She gave it to me.*

9.8 | Pronouns in commands

When the command is *to do* something, the pronoun comes *after* the verb:

Donne-**le**-lui.   *Give it to him.*
Montrez-**lui** votre passeport.   *Show him your passport.*

When the command is *not to do* something (i.e. in the negative), the pronouns come *before* the verb:

Surtout, ne **le lui** dites pas!   *Be sure not to tell him.*
Ne **lui** dites rien.   *Don't say anything to her.*

Note: In commands **moi** and **toi** are used instead of *me* and *te* except when the command is in the negative:

Donnez-**moi** un kilo de tomates, s'il vous plaît.
Ne **me** regarde pas, comme ça!

10 | *y* and *en*

10.1 | *y*

Y, meaning 'there', is used instead of repeating the name of a place:

— Qu'est-ce qu'on achète à la pâtisserie?
— On **y** achète des gâteaux.
— Tu vas à Strasbourg cette semaine?
— Oui, j'**y** vais demain.

Y is also used to replace *à* or *dans* + a noun or phrase which does not refer to a person:

— Je pensais à partir plus tôt.   *I was thinking of leaving earlier.*
— Moi, j'**y** pensais aussi.   *I was also thinking of that.*

It is used in many everyday expressions, where it has no particular meaning:

Il **y** a ...   *There is, there are...*
Il **y** a deux ans ...   *Two years ago ...*
On **y** va?   *Let's go.*
J'**y** suis.   *I've got it; I'm with you.*
Ça **y** est!   *It's done; That's it.*
Vas-**y**! Allez-**y**!   *Go on! Come on!* (shouted at football matches etc
Je m'**y** connais.   *I'm well up on that.*
Je n'**y** peux rien.   *I can't do anything about it.*

10.2 en

En means 'some', 'any', 'of them' or 'of it':

Ce pâté est excellent. Tu **en** veux?   *... Do you want some?*
— Tu as du sucre?
— Oui, j'**en** ai.   *Yes, I've got some.*
— Est-ce qu'il y a du gâteau?
— Non, il n'y **en** a plus.   *There isn't any left.*
— Est-ce qu'il y a une banque près d'ici?
— Oui, il y **en** a une, rue Victor Hugo.   *There's one (of them) in the rue Victor Hugo.*
— Avez-vous des frères ou des sœurs?
— Non, je n'**en** ai pas.   *No, I haven't any (of them).*
— Il a acheté combien de disques?
— Il **en** a acheté cinq.   *He bought five (of them).*
— Avez-vous du jambon? J'**en** voudrais   *I'd like four slices (of it).*
quatre tranches.

Note: When an infinitive is used, **en** often goes in front of the infinitive:

Quoi! Tu vas encore acheter des
chaussures? Mais tu dois déjà **en** avoir   *You must have at least ten pairs*
au moins dix paires!   *(of them).*
Je veux lui **en** parler.   *I want to speak to her about it.*

It is often used to replace an expression beginning with *du, de la, de l'* or *des:*

— Est-ce qu'elle aura besoin d'une raquette de tennis?
— Oui, elle **en** aura sûrement besoin.
— Est-ce que votre fils a peur des chiens?
— Oui, il **en** a très peur.
— Quand est-ce qu'il est sorti de la banque?
— Il **en** est sorti à trois heures.
— Quand êtes-vous revenu de Paris?
— J'**en** suis revenu samedi dernier.

En is also used in the following expressions:

Je n'en sais rien.	*I don't know anything about it.*
J'en ai assez.	*I've had enough.*
J'en ai marre.	*I'm fed up.*
Où en étions-nous?	*Where were we?*
Je n'en peux plus.	*I can't do any more.*
Il y en a dix.	*There are ten of them.*
Il n'y en a pas.	*There aren't any.*
Je m'en vais.	*I'm off.*

Note: **En** is also used as a preposition to mean 'in' or 'by'. (*See* 13.3)

11 Relative pronouns

Relative pronouns are words like **qui, que** and **dont,** which link two parts of a sentence together and refer back to a noun or phrase in the first part of the sentence.

11.1 *qui*

Qui means 'who' when referring to people:

Voici l'infirmière **qui** travaille à la clinique à La Rochelle.

Qui means 'which' or 'that' when referring to things or places:

C'est un petit hôtel **qui** ne coûte pas cher.
Le mistral est un vent du nord **qui** souffle en Provence.

In each of the above sentences, **qui** has replaced a noun *(l'infirmière, un petit hôtel, le mistral)* which would otherwise stand as the subject of the verb which comes after **qui**.

Qui is also used after prepositions, when referring to people. Notice that it is never shortened before a word beginning with a vowel (unlike **que**):

Ce sont les gens avec **qui** il travaille.
Tu connais le garçon à **qui** elle parle?
C'est la famille chez **qui** j'ai passé mes vacances, l'année dernière.

Note: If **qui** is used in a sentence in the Perfect Tense with *être,* the past participle must agree with the noun or phrase which **qui** has replaced:

Ma sœur, **qui** est allée aux États-Unis, connaît très bien la France.
Ce sont les garçons **qui** sont venus à la piscine, n'est-ce pas?

11.2 *que*

Que means 'that' or 'which' and is sometimes left out in English. **Que** must never be omitted in French:

C'est un nouveau disque **que** je viens d'acheter.
C'est le garçon **que** nous avons rencontré à la discothèque.

Que can refer back to people or things. In the above sentences **que** has replaced *un nouveau disque* and *le garçon*. In both cases, these are the object of the verb which follows **que**. (The subjects are *je* and *nous*).

If the following word begins with a vowel, **que** is shortened to **qu'**:

La voiture **qu'**il conduit est une Renault.

Note: If **que** is used in a sentence in the Perfect Tense with *avoir*, the past participle must agree with the word that **que** refers back to (*See also* 18.2):

La voiture **qu'**il a achetée est une Citroën.

Les chaussures **qu'**elle a achetées ont coûté 500 francs.

11.3 *dont*

Dont means 'whose', 'of whom', 'of which', 'from which', 'about whom', 'about which'. It is used quite a lot in conversational French to refer back to *what* or *whom* you were talking about:

C'est le livre **dont** je te parlais.	*It's the book I was telling you about.*
Voilà le garçon **dont** elle parlait.	*There's the boy she was talking about.*
C'est une maladie **dont** on peut mourir.	*It's a disease from which you can die.*

Dont is used instead of *qui* or *que* with verbs which must be followed by *de* (*See* 29.3):

C'est le livre **dont** elle a besoin pour faire ses devoirs.	*It's the book she needs for her homework.*
C'est un animal **dont** tout le monde a peur.	*It's an animal that everyone is afraid of.*
C'est quelque chose **dont** on se sert pour ouvrir les boîtes.	*It's something that you use for opening tins.*

Note: **Dont** never changes its form and can refer to people or things, which are masculine, feminine, singular or plural.

11.4 *ce qui, ce que, ce dont*

These expressions are used when there is no noun or phrase to refer back to. They mean 'what', 'which' or 'that which':

Ce qui est important c'est de trouver un terrain de camping.	*What's important is to find a campsite.*
Ce qui me plaît en France c'est que les cafés sont ouverts toute la journée.	*What appeals to me in France is that the cafés are open all day.*
Dites-moi **ce que** vous avez fait à Paris.	*Tell me what you did in Paris.*
C'est exactement **ce dont** j'ai besoin.	*It's exactly what I need.*

Ce qui and ce que are often used after *tout* to mean 'everything that', 'all that':

Tout **ce qui** brille n'est pas or.	*All that glitters is not gold.*
Mangez tout **ce que** vous voulez.	*Eat as much as you want.*
C'est tout **ce qu**'il y a.	*That's all there is.*
Ce livre vous expliquera tout **ce qu**'il faut savoir.	*This book will explain (to you) all you need to know.*

11.5 *lequel, laquelle* etc.

masculine singular	feminine singular	masculine plural	feminine plural
lequel	**laquelle**	**lesquels**	**lesquelles**

These words mean 'which' and are used after prepositions to refer to things but not people. They often come *after* a noun and must agree with it:

C'est le film dans **lequel** Catherine Deneuve joue le rôle d'une politicienne.	*It's the film in which Catherine Deneuve plays the part of a politician.*
— Donne-moi la valise.	— *Give me the case.*
— **Laquelle?**	— *Which one?*
C'est mon oncle qui m'a donné les 10 000 francs, avec **lesquels** je me suis offert un voyage en Italie.	*It was my uncle who gave me the 10,000 francs, with which I treated myself to a holiday in Italy.*
Les vacances pendant **lesquelles** j'ai beaucoup voyagé, étaient les meilleures.	*The holidays in which I travelled around a lot were the best.*

After the prepositions *à* and *de,* the following forms are used:

masculine singular	feminine singular	masculine plural	feminine plural
auquel	**à laquelle**	**auxquels**	**auxquelles**
duquel	**de laquelle**	**desquels**	**desquelles**

Le bureau d'objets trouvés est un bureau **auquel** on peut s'adresser si on a perdu quelque chose.

C'est une invention grâce **à laquelle** on peut faire des calculs très rapidement.

C'est la place au milieu **de laquelle** se trouve l'Obélisque.

C'est le cinéma près **duquel** il y a un grand café.

12 Indefinite adjectives and pronouns

12.1 *autre*

Autre, meaning 'other' or 'another', can be used as an adjective or a pronoun:

Où sont les **autres?**	*Where are the others?*	(pronoun)
Qui est l'**autre?**	*Who's the other one?*	(pronoun)
Je viendrai un **autre** jour.	*I'll come another day.*	(adjective)

12.2 *chaque* and *chacun*

i) **Chaque,** meaning 'each' or 'every', is an adjective which is invariable (It doesn't change form to agree with masculine or feminine nouns):

Chaque personne doit avoir une carte d'identité.
Chaque garçon devrait apprendre à faire la cuisine.

ii) **Chacun (chacune)** meaning 'each one', is a pronoun:

Chacun à son goût.   *Each (person) to his own taste.*

12.3 *même*

i) **Même,** meaning 'the same' or 'the very', is an adjective:

Nous avons les **mêmes** disques.   *We've got the same records.*
Il est arrivé ce jour **même.**   *He arrived on that very day.*

ii) **Même,** meaning 'even', is an adverb:

Il ne m'a **même** pas téléphoné.   *He didn't even phone me.*

12.4 *plusieurs*

Plusieurs, meaning 'several', is an adjective which is invariable:

Elle a voyagé dans **plusieurs** pays.
Il a acheté **plusieurs** chemises.

12.5 | quelque, quelques

Quelque, meaning 'some' or 'several', is an adjective:

On a invité **quelques** amis.   *We've invited some friends.*

Note also the following expressions:

quelqu'un	*someone*
quelque part	*somewhere*
quelque chose	*something*

12.6 | quelques-uns, quelques-unes

Quelques-uns (quelques-unes), meaning 'some' or 'some of them', is a pronoun:

Parmi ces enfants, il y en a **quelques-uns** qui n'ont jamais vu leurs parents.   *Amongst these children, there are some who have never seen their parents.*

12.7 | tout

masculine singular	feminine singular	masculine plural	feminine plural
tout	**toute**	**tous**	**toutes**

i) **Tout**, meaning 'all', 'the whole' or 'every' is usually used as an adjective and agrees with the noun that follows:

On a mangé **tout** le pain.	*We've eaten the whole loaf.*
Je suis resté sur la plage **toute** la journée.	*I stayed on the beach all day.*
On va en France **tous** les ans.	*We go to France every year.*
Dans **toutes** les régions de France on trouve un conseil régional.	*In every region of France there is a regional council.*

ii) **Tout**, meaning 'all' or 'everything', can sometimes be used as a pronoun. When this is the case, it doesn't change form:

On a **tout** vu.	*We've seen everything.*
Tout est bien qui finit bien.	*All's well that ends well.*

iii) Useful expressions with **tout:**

tout le monde	*everyone*
tout à fait	*absolutely, completely*
pas du tout	*not at all*
tous (toutes) les deux	*both*
tout à coup	*suddenly*
tout de suite	*straightaway, immediately*
à tout prix	*at all costs*

13 Prepositions

13.1 *à ('to' or 'at')*

masculine singular	feminine singular	before a vowel	plural
au	**à la**	**à l'**	**aux**

Il va **au** parc.
Si on allait **à la** piscine?
Je l'ai vu **à l'**hôtel.
Ils sont allés **aux** magasins.

À can be used on its own with nouns which do not have an article, e.g. names of towns:

Elle va **à** Paris.

À can sometimes have a different meaning from 'to' or 'at', as in the following examples:

Le garçon **aux** cheveux blonds.	*... with blonde hair.*
au printemps	*in Spring*
à la campagne; **à la** montagne	*in the country; in the mountains*
au sous-sol; **au** premier étage	*in the basement; on the first floor*
à pied; **à** cheval	*on foot; on horseback*
Le train est arrivé **à l'**heure.	*... on time.*
Elle est très **à la** mode.	*... fashionable; in fashion.*
À mon avis ...	*In my opinion...*
Il ressemble **à** son frère.	*He looks like his brother.*
Elle a volé 100 francs **à la** caisse.	*She stole 100 francs from the till.*
Il a emprunté 50 francs **à** sa sœur.	*He's borrowed 50 francs from his sister.*
Je joue **au** tennis.	*I play tennis.*
Le disque est **à** Suzanne.	*The record is Susan's.*

When used with a noun, **à** tells you what an object is used for:

une tasse **à** café	*a coffee cup*
une cuillère **à** soupe	*a soup spoon*
une brosse **à** dents	*a toothbrush*
une machine **à** laver	*a washing machine*
une machine **à** écrire	*a typewriter*

13.2 *de* ('of' or 'from')

masculine singular	feminine singular	before a vowel	plural
du	**de la**	**de l'**	**des**

Pour aller **du** centre-ville à la gare, c'est loin?
C'est un vin **de la** région.
Est-ce qu'ils sont rentrés **de l'**école?
Elle est partie **des** États-Unis samedi dernier.

De can be used on its own with nouns which do not have an article e.g. names and towns:

Elle vient **de** Calais.

Notice the following uses of **de** (*See also* 4.4):

le train **de** Lyon	*the train to (or from)* Lyon*
Rien **de** spécial.	*Nothing special.*
C'est à moi **de** payer.	*It's my turn to pay.*
une bouteille **de** limonade	*a bottle of lemonade*
plus **de** cinquante personnes	*more than fifty people*
pour les moins **de** vingt ans	*for the under twenties*
Est-ce qu'il y a quelqu'un **d'**autre?	*... anyone else?*
Il était couvert **de** neige.	*It was covered with snow.*

* If it is necessary to specify whether the train is arriving from or heading towards Lyon, use the following:

Le train, **en provenance de** Lyon ...	*(arriving from)*
Le train, **à destination de** Lyon ...	*(heading towards)*

13.3   *en* ('in', 'by', 'to', 'made of')

En is often used with the names of countries and regions (*See also* 13.7):

Strasbourg se trouve **en** Alsace.
Nous passons nos vacances **en** Italie.
Je vais **en** France.

It is used with most means of transport:

en autobus	*by bus*	*****en moto**	*by motorbike*
en autocar	*by coach*	**en taxi**	*by taxi*
en avion	*by plane*	*****en vélo**	*by bike*
en bateau	*by boat*	*****en vélomoteur**	*by moped*
en camion	*by lorry*	**en voiture**	*by car*

* **à** is also used, but **en** is becoming more and more common.

It is used to describe what something is made of:

C'est **en** cuir ou **en** plastique?	*Is it leather or plastic?*
des fleurs **en** papier	*paper flowers*
Elle est **en** coton ou **en** nylon?	*Is it cotton or nylon?*

Notice the following additional uses:

en 1789	*in 1789*
Le film est **en** version originale,	*... with the original soundtrack,*
mais il est sous-titré **en** anglais.	*but it is sub-titled in English.*
On fait les vendanges **en** octobre.	*The grapes are picked in October.*
en automne, **en** hiver, **en** été	*in Autumn, in Winter, in Summer*

13.4   *par* ('by')

par le train	*by train*
par le métro	*by métro*
une fois **par** semaine	*once a week*
par exemple	*for example*

pour ('for')

C'est bien le train **pour** Grenoble?	*... for (going to) ...*
Dix **pour** cent.	*Ten per cent.*
Elle n'est pas assez âgée **pour** avoir son permis.	*She's not old enough to have her driving licence.*
Je suis trop âgé **pour** faire du ski.	*I'm too old to go skiing.*
Vous allez en France **pour** combien de temps?	*How long are you going to France for?* (future time)

But note the following:

Mon frère habite à Toulouse **depuis** deux ans.	*My brother has lived in Toulouse for two years.*
Mes parents y sont restés **pendant** quinze jours.	*My parents stayed there for a fortnight.*

13.6 Common prepositions describing position

contre	*against*	**à côté de**	*next to*
dans	*in*	**au-dessus de**	*above*
devant	*in front of*	**au-dessous de**	*below*
derrière	*behind*	**à l'intérieur de**	*inside*
entre	*between*	**au milieu de**	*in the middle of*
sous	*under*	**en face de**	*opposite*
sur	*on*	**loin de**	*far from*
au bout de	*at the end of*	**près de**	*near*
au coin de	*at the corner of*		

Le cinéma est **en face du** supermarché.
Le théâtre est **à côté de** l'hôtel de ville.
L'office de tourisme est **près de la** gare.
On a volé **au-dessus de** Paris.

Notice the use of **prendre dans**:

Il a **pris** le livre **dans** la bibliothèque.	*He took the book from (in) the bookcase.*

13.7 Prepositions with countries and towns

The general rule is that **à** is used with names of towns to mean both 'in' and 'to':

Je travaille **à** Paris.
Elle va **à** La Rochelle.

If the name of the town has *le* before it, e.g. Le Havre, Le Mans, then **au** is used:

Ils vont **au** Havre.

En is used with names of feminine countries (most countries are feminine) and masculine countries beginning with a vowel. It can mean 'in' or 'to':

Il y a beaucoup de touristes **en** France en été.
Nous allons **en** Hongrie cette année.

Au or **aux** is used with other masculine countries:

au Canada	**au** Japon
au Danemark	**au** Luxembourg
aux États-Unis	**au** Pays de Galles

De is used with towns and feminine countries to mean 'of' or 'from':

Elle vient **de** Belgique.
Les vins **de** Bordeaux.

Du or **des** is used with masculine countries and when the name of the town has *le* before it:

Les 24 heures **du** Mans.   (Le Mans)
Ils viennent **des** États-Unis.   (les États-Unis *m.pl.*)

13.8 Translating verbs with prepositions

Notice how the following French verbs include a preposition in their meaning (unlike their English equivalents):

Il **cherche** un emploi.	*He's looking for a job.*
Tu l'as **payé** combien?	*How much did you pay for it?*
Elle **écoute** la radio.	*She's listening to the radio.*
Vous **attendez** l'autobus depuis longtemps?	*Have you been waiting for the bus for long?*

Note: Some verbs must be followed by **à** or **de** (*See* 29.2–29.4)

14 Numbers, dates, time and measurement

14.1 Numbers

1	un, une	41	quarante et un
2	deux	42	quarante-deux *etc.*
3	trois	50	cinquante
4	quatre	51	cinquante et un
5	cinq	52	cinquante-deux *etc.*
6	six	60	soixante
7	sept	61	soixante et un
8	huit	62	soixante-deux *etc.*
9	neuf	70	soixante-dix
10	dix	71	soixante et onze
11	onze	72	soixante-douze *etc.*
12	douze	80	quatre-vingts
13	treize	81	quatre-vingt-un
14	quatorze	82	quatre-vingt-deux *etc.*
15	quinze	90	quatre-vingt-dix
16	seize	91	quatre-vingt-onze *etc.*
17	dix-sept	100	cent
18	dix-huit	101	cent un *etc.*
19	dix-neuf	200	deux cents
20	vingt	201	deux cent un *etc.*
21	vingt et un	500	cinq cents
22	vingt-deux *etc.*	1,000	mille
30	trente	1,001	mille un *etc.*
31	trente et un	2,000	deux mille
32	trente-deux *etc.*	1,000,000	un million
40	quarante		

¼ un quart   ⅓ un tiers   ½ un demi*   ¾ trois-quarts

* **La moitié** is used to mean 'the *or* a half'. Notice the following differences of use:

Quelle est **la moitié** de quatre?

Je passe **la moitié** de mon temps à Paris.

Il a six ans et **demi**.

Note: Telephone numbers are read out in groups of two or three digits, e.g. 888. 92. 17:

huit cent quatre-vingt-huit   quatre-vingt douze   dix-sept

14.2 | 'First', 'second', 'third' etc.

1st premier, première (1er)	**8th** huitième (8e)	**15th** quinzième (15e)
2nd deuxième (2e)	**9th** neuvième (9e)	**16th** seizième (16e)
3rd troisième (3e)	**10th** dixième (10e)	**17th** dix-septième (17e)
4th quatrième (4e)	**11th** onzième (11e)	**18th** dix-huitième (18e)
5th cinquième (5e)	**12th** douzième (12e)	**19th** dix-neuvième (19e)
6th sixième (6e)	**13th** treizième (13e)	**20th** vingtième (20e)
7th septième (7e)	**14th** quatorzième (14e)	**21st** vingt et unième (21e) *etc.*

Note:

— that **premier** has a different masculine and feminine form:

le **premier** jour des vacances

la **première** année de ma vie

— the word order in the following phrase:

les **deux premières** personnes *the first two people*

— that **seconde** is occasionally found instead of *deuxième* e.g. for school years:

J'étais en troisième, mais l'année prochaine, je serai en **seconde**.

14.3 | Days of the week

Les jours de la semaine

lundi	*Monday*	**vendredi**	*Friday*
mardi	*Tuesday*	**samedi**	*Saturday*
mercredi	*Wednesday*	**dimanche**	*Sunday*
jeudi	*Thursday*		

Days of the week are normally written with a small letter. No separate word for 'on' is needed:

J'arriverai **samedi** soir.   *I will arrive on Saturday evening.*

Vendredi dernier, il est allé à Orléans.   *Last Friday he went to Orléans.*

Le before the day of the week implies that something happens *every* Monday, *every* Friday etc.:

Le lundi, j'ai un cours de piano.   *On Mondays I have a piano lesson.*

Useful expressions:

aujourd'hui	*today*	**avant-hier**	*the day before yesterday*
hier	*yesterday*	**après-demain**	*the day after tomorrow*
demain	*tomorrow*		

14.4 Months and seasons

Les mois de l'année

janvier	*January*	**juillet**	*July*
février	*February*	**août**	*August*
mars	*March*	**septembre**	*September*
avril	*April*	**octobre**	*October*
mai	*May*	**novembre**	*November*
juin	*June*	**décembre**	*December*

Les saisons

le (au) printemps	*(in) Spring*	**l' (en) automne**	*(in) Autumn*
l' (en) été	*(in) Summer*	**l' (en) hiver**	*(in) Winter*

The months of the year and the seasons are normally written with a small letter.
Use **en** or **au mois de** to say 'in' a particular month:

Mon anniversaire est **en** septembre. *My birthday is in September.*

Je pars en vacances **au mois de** juin.

On fait les vendanges **aux mois de** septembre et **d'**octobre.

14.5 Dates

le premier janvier	*January 1st*	**le trois mars**	*March 3rd*
le deux février	*February 2nd*	**le quatre avril**	*April 4th*
		etc.	

No separate word for 'on' is needed:

Nous rentrons en Angleterre **le vingt-trois août.**

With years, **en** is used to mean 'in':

En 1983 ... (**En** dix-neuf cent quatre-vingt-trois ...)

Useful expressions:

Quel jour sommes-nous?	*What day is it?*
On est mardi.	*It's Tuesday.*
Quelle est la date?	*What is the date?*
C'est le quinze mai.	*It's the 15th of May.*
C'est quand, votre anniversaire?	*When's your birthday?*
C'est le 5 octobre.	*It's the 5th of October.*
Quelle est la date de votre arrivée en France?	*What's the date of your arrival in France?*

The hours

Il est une heure.

Il est deux heures.

Minutes past the hour

Il est trois heures cinq.

Il est trois heures dix.

Minutes to the hour

Il est quatre heures
moins cinq.

Il est quatre heures
moins dix.

Quarter and half hours

Il est trois heures
et quart.

Il est trois heures
et demie.

Il est quatre heures
moins le quart.

a.m. and p.m.

Il est neuf heures du matin.	*9.00 a.m.*
Il est cinq heures de l'après-midi.	*5.00 p.m.*
Il est dix heures du soir.	*10.00 p.m.*

Midday and midnight

Il est midi.	*12 noon*
Il est minuit.	*12 midnight*
Il est midi cinq.	*12.05 p.m.*
Il est midi et demi.	*12.30 p.m.*
Il est minuit et demi.	*12.30 a.m.*

24 hour clock

Il est treize heures.	*13.00*
Il est quatorze heures cinq.	*14.05*
Il est quinze heures quinze.	*15.15*
Il est seize heures trente.	*16.30*
Il est dix-sept heures quarante-cinq.	*17.45*

Useful expressions:

Quelle heure est-il?	*What time is it?*
Vous avez **l'heure,** s'il vous plaît?	*Have you got the time please?*
Ça commence **à quelle heure?**	*When does it begin?*
Ça commence **à neuf heures précises.**	*It begins at 9 o'clock sharp.*
Il est **cinq heures juste.**	*It's exactly 5 o'clock.*
Je viendrai te chercher **vers huit heures.**	*I'll come and collect you at around 8 o'clock.*
Je serai là **dans une demi-heure.**	*I'll be there in half an hour.*
Le train est arrivé **à l'heure.**	*The train arrived on time.*
Il est arrivé **tôt.**	*He arrived early.*
Elle s'est réveillée **de bonne heure.**	*She woke up early.*
D'habitude, il arrive **tard.**	*Usually he arrives late.*
Dix minutes **de retard.**	*Ten minutes delay.*

14.7 Time of day

le matin	*(in) the morning*
l'heure du déjeuner	*lunch-hour*
l'après-midi	*(in) the afternoon*
la pause-café	*coffee break*
le soir	*(in) the evening*
la nuit	*(in) the night*

14.8 Quantity

Approximate numbers are formed by adding -**aine** to the number:

une **dizaine**	*about ten*
une **douzaine**	*a dozen*
une **quinzaine**	*about fifteen days* (= a fortnight)
une **vingtaine**	*about twenty*

Half and quarters:

un **demi**	*half* (used with measures and numbers)
une **demi-heure**	*half an hour*
un **demi** (-litre)	*half (a litre)* (used for beer)
un **demi-kilo**	*half a kilo*
la **moitié**	*half* (in a general sense)
la **moitié de la journée**	*half the day*
Elle travaille **à mi-temps**.	*She works part-time.*
un **quart**	*quarter*

Expressions of quantity:

beaucoup de	*a lot of, many*
(un) **peu de**	*a little of, few*
trop de	*too many, too much*
(pas) **assez de**	*(not) enough of*
plusieurs	*several*
la **plupart de**	*most of*

14.9 Measurement

100 grammes	*100 grams*	un **centimètre**	*a centimetre*
une **livre**	*a pound* (weight)	un **mètre**	*a metre*
un **demi-kilo**	*half a kilo*	**500 mètres**	*500 metres*
un **kilo**	*a kilo*	un **kilomètre**	*a kilometre*
un **litre**	*a litre* (used for liquids)	un **mile**	*mile*

Useful expressions:

Tu mesures combien?	*How tall are you?*
Je mesure un mètre soixante-dix.	*I'm one metre seventy* (approx. 5ft. 3 ins).
Tu pèses combien?	*How much do you weigh?*
Environ 57 kilos.	*About 57 kilos* (approx. 9 stone)
Quelle est votre taille?	*What is your size?* (clothing)
C'est quelle pointure?	*What shoe size?*

14.10 Distance

C'est tout près.	*It's very near.*
C'est près de ...	*It's near the ...*
C'est assez loin.	*It's quite a way.*
C'est loin.	*It's some distance.*
C'est très loin.	*It's a very long way away.*
C'est près d'ici?	*Is it near here?*
C'est loin?	*Is it far?*
C'est à 2 kilomètres.	*It's 2 kilometres away.*
C'est à dix minutes d'ici.	*It's ten minutes from here.*
C'est à 500 mètres environ.	*It's about 500 metres away.* (approx. one-third of a mile)

14.11 North, south, east, west

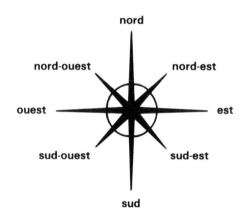

Lille est une ville **dans le nord** de la France.

Les Alpes se trouvent **dans le sud-est** de la France.

L'Espagne se trouve **au sud** de la France.

La Suisse se trouve **à l'est**.

J'habite à Rennes, à 344 km **à l'ouest** de Paris.

15 Words of general use

15.1 Expressions of time

i) General

après	*after*
aussitôt	*immediately*
avant	*before*
de temps en temps	*from time to time*
d'habitude	*usually*
encore	*again, still*
en même temps	*at the same time*
une fois (six fois)	*once (six times)*
jamais	*never*
pendant	*during*
pour la dernière fois	*for the last time*
quelquefois	*sometimes*
souvent	*often*
toujours	*always*
tout à l'heure	*presently, just now*
tout de suite	*straight away*

ii) Past

autrefois	*formerly*
l'autre jour	*the other day*
avant-hier	*the day before yesterday*
dans le temps	*in times past*
depuis	*since, for*
(On est là **depuis** deux jours)	*(We've been here for two days)*
en ce temps-là	*at that time*
hier	*yesterday*
il y a longtemps	*a long time ago*
il y a trois semaines	*three weeks ago*
le lendemain	*the following day*
quand j'étais petit(e)	*when I was small*
récemment	*recently*
samedi dernier	*last Saturday*
la semaine (l'année) dernière	*last week (year)*

iii) Present

actuellement	*at the present time*
aujourd'hui	*today*
de nos jours	*nowadays*
en ce moment	*at this moment*
maintenant	*now*

iv) Future

après-demain	*the day after tomorrow*
bientôt	*soon*
dans dix minutes	*in ten minutes time*
dans trois jours (ans)	*in three days (years)*
demain	*tomorrow*
l'année prochaine	*next year*
la semaine prochaine	*next week*
tout de suite	*straight away*
vendredi prochain	*next Friday*

15.2 Linking expressions

à la fin	*in the end*
à propos	*by the way*
ainsi	*thus*
alors	*in that case, then, so*
alors que	*whereas*
bref	*in short*
car	*for, because*
cependant	*however*
c'est-à-dire	*that's to say*
d'abord	*first, at first*
d'ailleurs	*moreover, besides*
déjà	*already*
de toute façon	*in any case*
donc	*therefore, so*
du moins	*at any rate*
et	*and*
et ... et	*both ... and*
en effet	*indeed, as a matter of fact*
en fait	*in fact*
en général	*in general*
enfin	*at last, finally*
ensuite	*then, next*
finalement	*finally*
lorsque	*when* (mainly in written French)

mais	but
malgré	in spite of
naturellement	of course
où	where
ou	or
parce que	because
par conséquent	as a result, consequently
peut-être	perhaps
pourtant	however
puis	then, next
quand	when
quand même	all the same
si	if
soit ... soit	either ... or
soudain	suddenly
surtout	above all
tandis que	while, whereas
tout à coup	suddenly

15.3 Describing location (*See also* 13.6)

ailleurs	elsewhere
au rez-de-chaussée	on the ground floor
au sous-sol	in the basement
au premier (deuxième) étage	on the first (second) floor
ici	here
là	there
là-bas	over there
nulle part	nowhere
partout	everywhere
quelque part	somewhere
dans la rue	in the street
au bout de	at the end of
au centre de	in the centre of
à droite	on the right
à gauche	on the left
tout droit	straight ahead
(dans) le nord	(in) the north
le sud	the south
l'est	the east
l'ouest	the west

Describing the weather

Present	**Quel temps fait-il?**	**Il fait beau**
Past (Imperfect)	**Quel temps faisait-il?**	**Il faisait froid**
Future	**Quel temps fera-t-il?**	**Il fera mauvais temps**

Present	**Il y a**	**du soleil**
Past (Imperfect)	**Il y avait**	**du brouillard**
Future	**Il y aura**	**du vent**

Present	**Il neige** **Il pleut**
Past (Imperfect)	**Il neigeait** *(It was snowing)* **Il pleuvait** *(It was raining)*
Past (Perfect)	**Il a neigé** *(It has snowed)* **Il a plu** *(It has rained)*
Future	**Il neigera** **Il pleuvra**

Other expressions:

une averse	*shower*	**le ciel**	*sky*
beau	*fine*	**commencer à (neiger)**	*to start (snowing)*
le brouillard	*fog*	**couvert**	*overcast*
la brume	*mist*	**un degré**	*degree*
cesser de (pleuvoir)	*to stop (raining)*	**un éclair**	*flash of lightning*
chaud	*hot*	**une éclaircie**	*sunny period*

frais	cool
froid	cold
geler	to freeze
gris	grey
mauvais	bad
un nuage	cloud
nuageux	cloudy
à l'ombre	in the shade
un orage	storm
la pluie	rain
la température	temperature
le temps	weather
le tonnerre	thunder
variable	changeable
le vent	wind

16 Parts of the body

16.1 le, la, l', les + parts of the body

Le, la, l', les are normally used with a part of the body instead of *mon, ma, mes* etc.:

Elle ferma **les yeux.**
She closed her eyes.

Ouvrez **la bouche** encore un peu, s'il vous plaît.
Open your mouth a little wider please.

16.2 Reflexive verbs + parts of the body

Reflexive verbs are often used when referring to a part of the body:

Il **se lave** les cheveux.
He's washing his hair.

Je **me coupe** les ongles.
I'm cutting my nails.

When used with a part of the body, the reflexive pronoun *(me, te, se, nous, vous)* acts as the *indirect object* (the part of the body is the *direct object*). For this reason, when used in the Perfect Tense, the past participle doesn't agree with the subject:

Elle **s'est coupé** le doigt.
She cut her finger.

Ils **se sont brossé** les dents.
They've brushed their teeth.

16.3 Indirect object pronouns + parts of the body

Notice that when the subject of the verb and the owner of the part of the body are different, you can't use a reflexive verb, but you can use an **indirect object pronoun** to indicate the owner of the part of the body:

On **lui** a mis la jambe dans le plâtre.	*They put his leg in plaster.*
Ils **lui** ont cassé le bras.	*They broke her arm.*

16.4 Describing pain or feeling

The preposition **à** + part of the body is normally used:

J'ai mal **aux yeux**.	*My eyes are hurting.*
Il a mal **à la tête**.	*He has a headache.*
J'ai froid **aux pieds**.	*My feet are cold.*
Elle a froid **aux mains**.	*Her hands are cold.*
Il s'est fait mal **au genou**.	*He's hurt his knee.*

16.5 Describing appearance

The definite article is not always needed when an adjective is used to describe a part of the body, particularly when the adjective comes before the noun:

Il a **un gros nez**.	*He's got a big nose.*
Elle a **de petits pieds**.	*She has small feet.*
Le bébé a **de grands yeux bleus**.	*The baby has big blue eyes.*
Il a **le visage rond**.	*He has a round face.*
C'est la dame **aux cheveux blonds**.	*It's the woman with blonde hair.*
C'est l'homme **à la barbe**.	*It's the man with the beard.*

17   The Present Tense

17.1   Use of the Present Tense

The Present Tense is used to describe what is happening *now,* at the present time.
In French, there is only one form of the Present Tense. *Il travaille* in French means 'he works', 'he is working' and 'he does work'.
The Present Tense is also used for things which happen *regularly,* even if they are not actually taking place now:

> D'habitude, je **passe** mes vacances en France.

17.2   How to form the Present Tense

i) Regular verbs form the Present Tense in one of three ways, depending on whether the infinitive of the verb ends in **-er**, **-re** or **-ir**:

jou**er**		répon**dre**		fin**ir**	
je	jou**e**	je	répon**ds**	je	fin**is**
tu	jou**es**	tu	répon**ds**	tu	fin**is**
il		il		il	
elle	jou**e**	elle	répon**d**	elle	fin**it**
on		on		on	
nous	jou**ons**	nous	répon**dons**	nous	fin**issons**
vous	jou**ez**	vous	répon**dez**	vous	fin**issez**
ils		ils		ils	
elles	jou**ent**	elles	répon**dent**	elles	fin**issent**

ii) **Irregular verbs**

Many commonly used French verbs are irregular, particularly in the Present Tense. Note in particular the following:

aller	**devoir**	**prendre**
avoir	**dire**	**savoir**
boire	**être**	**venir**
comprendre	**faire**	**voir**
connaître	**mettre**	**vouloir**
croire	**pouvoir**	

Some of these are very irregular, like **avoir** and **être**. Some are only slightly irregular, like **prendre** and **comprendre**. The most common irregular verbs are listed in the verb table on pages 110-127.

17.3 The Present Tense of *avoir* and *être*

Avoir and **être** are both used as auxiliary verbs in the Perfect Tense. Hence, the Present Tense of these two verbs is frequently used:

avoir	*to have*				être	*to be*		
j'	ai	nous	avons		je	suis	nous	sommes
tu	as	vous	avez		tu	es	vous	êtes
il		ils			il		ils	
elle }	a	elles }	ont		elle }	est	elles }	sont
on					on			

17.4 Imperative or command form

To tell someone *to do* something in French, you use the **imperative** or **command form**:

Attends-moi!   *Wait for me!*
Regardez ça!   *Look at that!*

You use the imperative form of *nous* to suggest doing something:

Allons au cinéma, ce soir!   *Let's go to the cinema tonight!*

It is very easy to form the imperative of regular verbs:

	Present Tense	*change needed*	*imperative*
-**er** verbs	tu regardes	~~tu~~ regardes*	**regarde!**
e.g.	vous regardez	~~vous~~ regardez	**regardez!**
regarder	nous regardons	~~nous~~ regardons	**regardons!**
-**re** verbs	tu attends	~~tu~~ attends	**attends!**
e.g.	vous attendez	~~vous~~ attendez	**attendez!**
attendre	nous attendons	~~nous~~ attendons	**attendons!**
-**ir** verbs	tu finis	~~tu~~ finis	**finis!**
e.g.	vous finissez	~~vous~~ finissez	**finissez!**
finir	nous finissons	~~nous~~ finissons	**finissons!**

* The final -**s** remains when the command is followed by a pronoun beginning with a vowel:

Vas-y!   Manges-en!

Notice that the command form is frequently used in the negative:

Ne **faites** pas ça!	*Don't do that!*
Ne **touche** à rien!	*Don't touch anything!*
Ne me **parle** pas comme ça!	*Don't speak to me like that!*
Ne me **quitte** pas!	*Don't leave me!*

The imperative form is often found in recipes:

Mélangez dans un saladier le lait, les yaourts et le jus de citron.

But in instructions for sewing and knitting patterns or for do-it-yourself ideas the infinitive is frequently used:

Fixer au mur, puis **passer** deux couches de peinture de couleur rouge.

18 The Perfect Tense

18.1 Use of the Perfect Tense

The Perfect Tense is the most commonly used of the past tenses. It is frequently used in conversation and letters. It describes an action which is completed and is no longer happening. Often, the action described happened once only. *Elle a joué* in French can mean either 'she played' or 'she has played':

L'année dernière, j'**ai passé** mes vacances à Bordeaux.

Un jour, on **a fait** une excursion à Biarritz.

Pendant les vacances, Jean et Nicole **sont venus** me voir.

The Perfect Tense is made up of two parts: an **auxiliary verb** (either **avoir** or **être**) and a **past participle**.

18.2 The Perfect Tense with *avoir*

Most verbs form the Perfect Tense with **avoir**.

i) Regular verbs

The past participle of regular verbs is formed as follows:

-**er** verbs ⟶ **é**   -**re** verbs ⟶ **u**   -**ir** verbs ⟶ **i**

Perfect Tense of regular verbs

manger			perdre			choisir		
j' ai			j' ai			j' ai		
tu as			tu as			tu as		
il			il			il		
elle $\}$ a			elle $\}$ a			elle $\}$ a		
on	mangé		on	perdu		on	choisi	
nous avons			nous avons			nous avons		
vous avez			vous avez			vous avez		
ils			ils			ils		
elles $\}$ ont			elles $\}$ ont			elles $\}$ ont		

ii) Irregular verbs

Many common verbs have irregular past participles. Here are some of the most important ones:

avoir	→ eu		faire	→ fait
boire	→ bu		mettre	→ mis
comprendre	→ compris		pouvoir	→ pu
connaître	→ connu		prendre	→ pris
croire	→ cru		savoir	→ su
devoir	→ dû		venir	→ venu
dire	→ dit		voir	→ vu
être	→ été		vouloir	→ voulu

These and others are listed in the verb table on pages 110-127.

iii) Agreement of the past participle

If there is a direct object, which comes before the *avoir* part of the Perfect Tense, then the past participle must agree with the direct object. This is most common with pronouns:

— Tu as vu Marc en ville?
— Non, je ne l'ai pas vu. *(masculine singular)*
— J'aime bien ta robe. Où l'as-tu achetée? *(feminine singular)*
— Tu as perdu tes gants?
— Oui, je crois que je **les** ai perdu**s** dans le restaurant. *(masculine plural)*
— Avez-vous acheté vos chaussures de ski?
— Non, je **les** ai lou**ées**. *(feminine plural)*

It can also occur with nouns, especially after *que, combien* and *quel:*

> Voilà **la maison** que M. et Mme Lebrun ont achetée.
>
> Combien de **timbres** as-tu achetés?
>
> Quelles **chaussettes** a-t-il mises?

Note: The agreement is rarely noticeable in spoken French, except in the case of *faire* (**faite** etc.) and *mettre* (**mise** etc.).

18.3 | The Perfect Tense with *être*

i) Sixteen verbs, mostly verbs of movement, like *aller, partir* etc. form the Perfect Tense with **être**. They are most easily remembered in pairs which are opposite or nearly opposite in meaning:

aller *to go*	⟶	**allé**
venir *to come*	⟶	**venu**
(also revenir, *to return*	⟶	**revenu**
and devenir, *to become)*	⟶	**devenu**
arriver *to arrive*	⟶	**arrivé**
partir *to leave*	⟶	**parti**
sortir *to go out*	⟶	**sorti**
entrer *to enter*	⟶	**entré**
(also rentrer, *to get back home)*	⟶	**rentré**
monter *to go upstairs*	⟶	**monté**
descendre *to go downstairs*	⟶	**descendu**
naître *to be born*	⟶	**né**
mourir *to die*	⟶	**mort**
rester *to stay*	⟶	**resté**
tomber *to fall*	⟶	**tombé**
retourner *to return*	⟶	**retourné**

All reflexive verbs form the Perfect Tense with **être** *(see* 25.4).

ii) Agreement of the past participle

The past participle must agree with the subject of the verb:

Perfect Tense of **aller**				
je suis	**allé(e)**	nous	sommes	**allé(e)s**
tu es	**allé(e)**	vous	êtes	**allé(e)(s)**
il est	**allé**	ils	sont	**allés**
elle est	**allée**	elles	sont	**allées**
on est	**allé**			

If the **e** is in brackets, only add it if the subject is feminine.
If the **s** is in brackets, only add it if the subject is plural.

Tu es allé au cinéma hier, Jean?

Tu es allée au cinéma hier, Nicole?

Vous êtes allé au cinéma hier, Monsieur?

Vous êtes allée au cinéma hier, Madame?

Vous êtes allés au cinéma hier, Jean et Pierre?

Vous êtes allées au cinéma hier, Nicole et Sylvie?

18.4 Verbs with two meanings

The three verbs **monter, descendre** and **sortir** are sometimes used with a direct object, which changes the meaning slightly. When this happens, they form the Perfect Tense with *avoir:*

Je **suis** monté(e).	*I went upstairs.*
Tu **as** monté les valises?	*Did you take the cases up?*
Il **est** descendu.	*He went downstairs.*
Avez-vous descendu les bagages?	*Have you brought the luggage down?*
Elle **est** sortie.	*She went out.*
Ils **ont** sorti les skis.	*They've got the skis out.*

19 The Imperfect Tense

19.1 Use of the Imperfect Tense

The Imperfect Tense is used to describe something that *used to happen* frequently or regularly in the past (a repeated action or habit in the past). It often translates 'used to' in English:

> Quand j'étais petit, j'**allais** chez mes grands-parents tous les week-ends.

It is also used for description in the past, particularly with weather:

> Il **faisait** beau tous les jours.
> Il **pleuvait** sans cesse.
> L'homme, comment **était**-il?
> Est-ce qu'il **portait** des lunettes?

C'était + adjective can be used to express an opinion:

> **C'était** bien, la journée à Paris?
> **C'était** magnifique.
> **C'était** affreux.

It is used to describe something that lasted for a long period, when there is no indication of when it started or when it finished:

> En ce temps-là, nous **habitions** à Marseille.

It is often used with a verb in the Perfect Tense or the Past Historic. The verb in the Imperfect Tense describes what was going on at the time when something else happened:

> — Que **faisiez**-vous quand l'accident est arrivé?
> — J'**étais** assise au café. Je **buvais** mon thé tout tranquillement, quand soudain la voiture bleue **est entrée** en collision avec la voiture rouge.

The Imperfect Tense is occasionally used to express a wish or suggestion:

> Si on **allait** au cinéma?   *How about going to the cinema?* (lit. *If we were to go to the cinema?*)
> Si seulement il **pouvait** être là.   *If only he could be there.*

How to form the Imperfect Tense

The Imperfect Tense is easy to form. Start with the *nous* form of the Present Tense:

nous allons

Take away the *nous* and the *-ons* ending:

all

This leaves the Imperfect stem to which the endings below are added:

endings for all verbs	verb in the Imperfect	être	manger
je -ais	j' allais	j' étais	je mangeais
tu -ais	tu allais	tu étais	tu mangeais
il elle }-ait on	il elle } allait on	il elle } était on	il elle } mangeait on
nous -ions	nous allions	nous étions	nous mangions
vous -iez	vous alliez	vous étiez	vous mangiez
ils elles }-aient	ils elles } allaient	ils elles } étaient	ils elles } mangeaient

Nearly all verbs form the Imperfect stem as described above. An important exception is **être**. The Imperfect stem is **ét**. Verbs like **manger, ranger, changer, nager** etc. take an extra **e** in the *nous* form of the Present Tense. This is to make the *g* sound soft (like a 'j' sound). The extra **e** isn't needed before *i* and *e*.
Similarly, with verbs like **commencer, lancer** etc., the final *c* becomes **ç** before *o* or *a* to make it sound soft. This gives **je commençais** but **nous commencions, vous commenciez**.

20 | The Past Historic Tense

20.1 | Use of the Past Historic Tense

The Past Historic Tense is another past tense and, like the Perfect Tense, it is used to describe *an action which is completed,* which *happened once only* or for *a defined period of time.*

However, it is only used in more formal written French, such as newspaper articles or novels. It is very rarely used in conversation or in personal letters:

Napoléon **fut** empereur des Français de 1804 à 1815.
Après la bataille de Waterloo, les Anglais l'**exilèrent** à Sainte-Hélène.
Il **mourut** en 1821.

20.2 | How to form the Past Historic Tense

It's useful to know how this tense is formed so that it can easily be recognised and understood. The stem is formed from the infinitive. The endings follow one of three main patterns:

all **-er** verbs have these endings	most regular **-ir** and **-re** verbs have these endings	a few regular **-oir** verbs and many irregular verbs have these endings
aller	**sortir**	**vouloir**
j' allai	je sortis	je voulus
tu allas	tu sortis	tu voulus
il elle } alla on	il elle } sortit on	il elle } voulut on
nous allâmes	nous sortîmes	nous voulûmes
vous allâtes	vous sortîtes	vous voulûtes
ils elles } allèrent	ils elles } sortirent	ils elles } voulurent

The following verbs have the same endings as the second group of verbs, listed above. They are listed here because the first part of the verb differs from the infinitive. Notice however that, in many cases, there is a similarity with the past participle (not in the case of **faire**, **voir** and **naître**):

comprendre	→ il **comprit**	mettre	→ il **mit**
conduire	→ il **conduisit**	naître	→ il **naquit**
construire	→ il **construisit**	prendre	→ il **prit**
dire	→ il **dit**	rire	→ il **rit**
écrire	→ il **écrivit**	voir	→ il **vit**
faire	→ il **fit**		

The following verbs have the same endings as the third group of verbs listed on page 79. Again, there is often a similarity with the past participle, but not in the case of **être**.

avoir	⟶ il **eut**		mourir	⟶ il **mourut**
boire	⟶ il **but**		pouvoir	⟶ il **put**
connaître	⟶ il **connut**		recevoir	⟶ il **reçut**
croire	⟶ il **crut**		savoir	⟶ il **sut**
devoir	⟶ il **dut**		vivre	⟶ il **vécut**
être	⟶ il **fut**			

Finally, the verbs **venir (revenir, devenir)** and **tenir** form the Past Historic in a completely different way:

venir			
je	**vins**	nous	**vînmes**
tu	**vins**	vous	**vîntes**
il elle on }	**vint**	ils elles }	**vinrent**

tenir			
je	**tins**	nous	**tînmes**
tu	**tins**	vous	**tîntes**
il elle on }	**tint**	ils elles }	**tinrent**

21 The Pluperfect Tense

21.1 Use of the Pluperfect Tense

The Pluperfect Tense is used to describe what had already taken place before something else happened or before a fixed point in time. In English, it is translated as 'had done', 'gone', 'happened' etc.

Il **était** déjà **parti** quand je suis arrivé.

Il m'**avait téléphoné** avant son arrivée à Paris.

Je lui **avais dit** que ce n'était pas un bon film, mais elle est allée le voir quand même.

21.2 | How to form the Pluperfect Tense

This tense is formed in a similar way to the Perfect Tense. The only difference is that the auxiliary verb (*avoir* or *être*) is in the Imperfect Tense. The same rules about agreement of the past participle apply to both tenses.

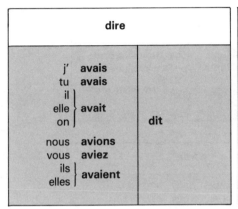

dire			arriver		
j'	avais		j'	étais	arrivé(e)
tu	avais		tu	étais	arrivé(e)
il			il	était	arrivé
elle	avait	dit	elle	était	arrivée
on			on	était	arrivé
nous	avions		nous	étions	arrivé(e)s
vous	aviez		vous	étiez	arrivé(e)(s)
ils	avaient		ils	étaient	arrivés
elles			elles	étaient	arrivées

22 | The Future Tense

22.1 | Use of the Future Tense

The Future Tense is used to describe what *will* (or *will not*) *take place* at some future time:

Qu'est-ce que tu **feras** après les vacances?
J'**irai** peut-être à Paris.
S'il fait beau demain, on **jouera** au tennis.
Si je gagne 100 000 francs, j'**achèterai** une nouvelle voiture.

The Future Tense must be used after *quand* if the idea of future time is implied:

Quand je **serai** à Paris, je **passerai** te voir.	*When I'm in Paris, I'll drop by to see you.*
Je lui **dirai** de vous téléphoner, quand il **rentrera** ce soir.	*I'll tell him to 'phone you when he comes in this evening.*

A simple way to refer to the Future, which is common in conversation, is to use the Present Tense of *aller* + the infinitive (*see* 26.8).

22.2 How to form the Future Tense

i) Most verbs form the Future Tense from the infinitive and a modified form of the Present Tense of **avoir**:

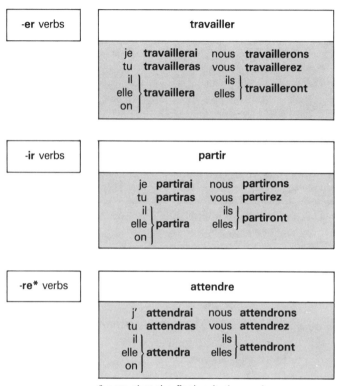

-er verbs	travailler		
	je **travaillerai**	nous	**travaillerons**
	tu **travailleras**	vous	**travaillerez**
	il elle } **travaillera** on	ils elles } **travailleront**	

-ir verbs	partir		
	je **partirai**	nous	**partirons**
	tu **partiras**	vous	**partirez**
	il elle } **partira** on	ils elles } **partiront**	

-re* verbs	attendre		
	j' **attendrai**	nous	**attendrons**
	tu **attendras**	vous	**attendrez**
	il elle } **attendra** on	ils elles } **attendront**	

* note that the final **-e** is dropped

ii) Some commonly used verbs are irregular in the way they form the Future stem (the part before the endings). However, the endings are always the same. Note in particular the following:

aller	⟶ j'**irai**	faire	⟶ je **ferai**	venir	⟶ je **viendrai**
avoir	⟶ j'**aurai**	recevoir	⟶ je **recevrai**	voir	⟶ je **verrai**
devoir	⟶ je **devrai**	pouvoir	⟶ je **pourrai**	vouloir	⟶ je **voudrai**
être	⟶ je **serai**	savoir	⟶ je **saurai**		

Some verbs, like *acheter* (j'**achèterai**), differ only slightly from the regular pattern. These are all listed in the verb table, pages 108-9.

23 The Conditional Tense

23.1 Use of the Conditional Tense

The Conditional Tense is often used when *asking for something*. It is more polite and less abrupt than using the Present Tense:

Je **voudrais** écouter ce disque, s'il vous plaît.
I would like ... (rather than 'I want...')

Pourriez-vous réparer cet appareil-photo, s'il vous plaît?
Could you ... (rather than 'Can you ...')

The Conditional is also used where 'would' or 'should' are used in English:

Pour la gare de Lyon, vous **devriez** prendre l'autobus numéro 16.   *(...you should take...)*

Tu ne crois pas qu'il **serait** mieux de partir en vacances en septembre plutôt qu'en août?   *(... it would be better ...)*

Notice that it is frequently used when referring to what *would* happen if a particular condition were fulfilled (with *si* + Imperfect Tense):

Si j'avais beaucoup d'argent, je **ferais** le tour du monde.

Si j'envoyais ce paquet aujourd'hui, quand est-ce qu'il **arriverait?**

Sauriez-vous quoi faire si la voiture tombait en panne?
Would you know what to do if the car broke down?

Note, however, that sometimes 'would' is used in English in the sense of 'used to'. If this is the case, then the Imperfect Tense must be used:

Quand il était jeune, il **allait** à la pêche tous les week-ends.
When he was young, he would (i.e. used to) go fishing every weekend.

The Conditional is also used to report what someone said when, at the time of speaking, the Future Tense was used. It therefore has the effect of 'putting the future in the past':

— Allô chérie, je **rentrerai** vers 7 heures ce soir.   (Future Tense)
— Ah, mais hier tu as dit que tu **rentrerais** vers 7 heures et tu es arrivé à 8 heures et demie seulement.   (Conditional Tense)

Mais vous m'avez dit que ma voiture **serait** prête à cinq heures!

La météo a dit qu'il **ferait** beau aujourd'hui, mais regarde comme il pleut.

23.2 | How to form the Conditional Tense

The Conditional Tense is formed by adding the Imperfect endings to the Future stem:

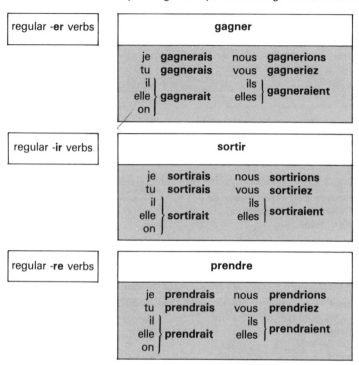

regular **-er** verbs	gagner		
	je **gagnerais**	nous **gagnerions**	
	tu **gagnerais**	vous **gagneriez**	
	il / elle / on **gagnerait**	ils / elles **gagneraient**	

regular **-ir** verbs	sortir		
	je **sortirais**	nous **sortirions**	
	tu **sortirais**	vous **sortiriez**	
	il / elle / on **sortirait**	ils / elles **sortiraient**	

regular **-re** verbs	prendre		
	je **prendrais**	nous **prendrions**	
	tu **prendrais**	vous **prendriez**	
	il / elle / on **prendrait**	ils / elles **prendraient**	

Verbs which are irregular in the Future Tense are also irregular in the Conditional Tense (See verb table pages 110-127).

23.3 | Past Conditional or Conditional Perfect

This is rarely used, except in 'If' sentences (see 24.3) and in the following useful expressions:

On **aurait dû** prendre l'avion.	*We should have taken the plane.*
J'**aurais dû** téléphoner avant de partir.	*I ought to have phoned before we left.*
Je l'**aurais cru.**	*I would have thought so.*
Il **aurait voulu** m'accompagner.	*He would have liked to come with me.*
Quand ses parents ont divorcé, Nicole est restée avec sa mère, mais elle **aurait préféré** être avec son père.	*... she would have preferred to be with her father.*
On **aurait pu** leur rendre visite.	*We could have visited them.*

84

24 'If' sentences

Sentences which contain two parts, one of which is an 'If' clause, normally follow one of the following patterns:

24.1 *Si* + Present Tense + Future Tense

Si tu **viens** à Paris cet été, on **pourra** se revoir.

If you come to Paris this summer, we can meet up again.

Si je **gagne** assez d'argent, je **partirai** en vacances de neige.

If I earn enough money, I'll go on a skiing holiday.

S'il pleut, je **resterai** à la maison.

If it rains, I'll stay at home.

24.2 *Si* + Imperfect Tense + Conditional Tense

S'il faisait plus chaud,on **pourrait** se baigner.

If it was warmer, we could go swimming.

Si j'**habitais** dans les Alpes, je **ferais** du ski tous les week-ends.

If I lived in the Alps, I'd go skiing every weekend.

Notice that the **si** clause does not always come first in the sentence:

Sauriez-vous quoi faire **s'il y avait** un accident de route?

Would you know what to do if there was a road accident?

24.3 *Si* + Pluperfect Tense + Conditional Perfect

Si tu m'**avais téléphoné** plus tôt, j'**aurais pu** venir.

If you had rung me earlier, I would have been able to come.

S'il avait su, il **serait venu** tout de suite.

If he had known, he would have come straight away.

Si elle **avait eu** assez d'argent, elle l'**aurait acheté**.

If she'd had enough money, she would have bought it.

Qu'est-ce que vous **auriez fait** hier, **si** vous **étiez allé** à Paris?

What would you have done yesterday, if you had gone to Paris?

25 Reflexive verbs

25.1 Reflexive verbs — general

Reflexive verbs are ones like **se laver** and **s'habiller** which require *a reflexive pronoun* to be added before the verb (see 25.2 opposite):

Je **me lave.**	*I get washed.*
Tu **te lèves?**	*Are you getting up?*
Il **se rase.**	*He gets shaved.*
Elle **s'habille.**	*She gets dressed.*
Nous **nous amusons** ici.	*We're enjoying ourselves here.*
Vous **vous reposez?**	*Are you having a rest?*
Ils **se disputent.**	*They're having an argument.*
Elles **s'entendent** bien.	*They get on well.*

They are just like ordinary verbs, apart from the extra (reflexive) pronoun. In fact, many reflexive verbs are regular *-er* verbs.

Some common reflexive verbs:

s' **amuser**	*to enjoy oneself*
s' **appeler**	*to be called*
s' **approcher (de)**	*to approach*
s' **arrêter**	*to stop*
se **baigner**	*to bathe*
se **brosser les dents**	*to clean your teeth*
se **coucher**	*to go to bed*
se **débrouiller**	*to sort things out, manage*
se **dépêcher**	*to be in a hurry*
se **demander**	*to ask oneself, to wonder*
se **déshabiller**	*to get undressed*
se **disputer (avec)**	*to have an argument*
s' **échapper**	*to escape*
s' **entendre (avec)**	*to get on (with)*
se **fâcher**	*to get angry*
se **faire mal**	*to hurt oneself*
s' **habiller**	*to get dressed*
s' **intéresser (à)**	*to be interested in*
se **laver**	*to get washed*
se **lever**	*to get up*
se **promener**	*to go for a walk*
se **raser**	*to shave*
se **reposer**	*to rest*

se réveiller	*to wake up*
se sauver	*to run away*
se trouver	*to be (situated)*

25.2 Reflexive pronouns

The pronouns (**me, te, se, nous, vous**) which come before the reflexive verb are called **reflexive pronouns**.

These can also be used to mean 'each other' or 'one another'. Many verbs can be made reflexive by adding a reflexive pronoun in front:

Quand est-ce qu'on va **se revoir**?	*When shall we see each other again?*
Ils **se regardaient**.	*They looked at each other.*
Il faut **se dire** "Au revoir".	*We'll have to say 'Goodbye'.*

25.3 Reflexive verbs — commands

Notice how to tell someone to *do* something (or *not to*), using the imperative form of reflexive verbs:

Lève-toi!	*Get up!*
Amusez-vous bien!	*Have a good time!*
Dépêchons-nous!	*Let's hurry!*
Ne **te fâche** pas!	*Don't get angry!*
Ne **vous approchez** pas!	*Don't come near!*
Ne **nous disputons** pas!	*Don't let's argue!*

25.4 Reflexive verbs in the Perfect Tense

Reflexive verbs form the Perfect Tense with **être**:

se réveiller			
je	me suis réveillé(e)	nous	nous sommes réveillé(e)s
tu	t'es réveillé(e)	vous	vous êtes réveillé(e)(s)
il	s'est réveillé	ils	se sont réveillés
elle	s'est réveillée	elles	se sont réveillées
on	s'est réveillé		

Reflexive verbs + parts of the body

Reflexive verbs are often used when referring to a part of the body:

Je **me suis coupé** le pied.	*I've cut my foot.*
Il **se brosse** les dents.	*He's cleaning his teeth.*
Elle **se lave** la tête.	*She's washing her hair.*

Note: When a reflexive verb is used with a part of the body in the Perfect Tense, the past participle doesn't agree with the subject. (This is because the reflexive pronoun acts as the indirect object in this instance and not the direct object):

Elle **s'est lavé** les mains avant de manger.

— Qu'est-ce qui ne va pas, Mademoiselle?
— Je **me suis coupé** le doigt.

26 Verbs: some special uses

26.1 *avoir*

The following expressions all use **avoir:**

avoir ... ans	*to be ... years old*
avoir besoin de	*to need*
avoir chaud	*to feel hot*
avoir de la chance	*to be lucky*
avoir envie de	*to wish, want*
avoir faim	*to be hungry*
avoir froid	*to feel cold*
avoir l'air (fatigué *etc.*)	*to look, seem (tired* etc.)
avoir le droit de	*to have the right to*
avoir lieu	*to take place*
avoir mal	*to have a pain*
avoir peur	*to be frightened*
avoir raison	*to be right*
avoir soif	*to be thirsty*
avoir tort	*to be wrong*

— Quel âge avez-vous?
— J'**ai** seize **ans.**

— Ça va? Tu **as l'air** triste.
— Bof, ça va ... mais j'**ai** un peu **mal** à la tête.   *... I've got a bit of a headache.*

26.2 | *être*

Être is used in the following useful expressions:

être en train de + infinitive	*to be in the middle of doing something*
être sur le point de + infinitive	*to be about to do something*
être content (obligé) de + infinitive	*to be happy (obliged) to do something*

Il **était en train de** déjeuner quand le téléphone a sonné.

J'**étais sur le point de** partir quand mes amis sont arrivés.

Je **serai** très **content de** vous voir à Paris.

On **est obligé de** rentrer à l'auberge de jeunesse avant minuit.

26.3 | *faire*

The following expressions all use **faire**:

faire des achats	*to do some shopping*
faire attention	*to be careful*
faire de l'auto-stop	*to hitch-hike*
faire du camping	*to go camping*
faire des courses	*to do the shopping*
faire la cuisine	*to do the cooking*
faire ses devoirs	*to do one's homework*
faire des économies	*to save (money)*
faire la lessive	*to do the washing*
faire le ménage	*to do the housework*
faire le plein	*to fill up (with petrol)*
faire une promenade	*to go for a walk*
faire du tourisme	*to go sightseeing, to travel around*
faire la vaisselle	*to do the washing up*
faire les valises	*to pack (the cases)*

The verb **faire** is also used to describe the weather:

— Quel temps **fait**-il?

— Il **fait** beau. (chaud/mauvais/froid *etc.*)

Notice how **faire** can be used with another verb in the sense of getting something done:

faire réparer quelque chose	*to get something repaired*

J'**ai fait réparer** mon appareil-photo.	*I've had my camera repaired.*
Ils **ont fait construire** une maison.	*They've had a house built.*

It can also be used with **voir** in the sense of 'to show':

— J'ai des photos de mon petit ami.

— **Fais voir.**   *Let's have a look.*

26.4 | *pouvoir* ('to be able', 'can', 'may')

Pouvoir (like *vouloir* and *devoir*) is sometimes called a *modal verb*. It is usually followed by a second verb, which must be in the infinitive:

Est-ce que vous **pouvez venir** chez nous, samedi soir? — *Can you come round on Saturday night?*

Ça **peut durer** longtemps. — *It might go on for a long time.*

Je n'en **peux** plus. — *I can't stand it any longer.*

On **peut faire** du ski dans les Pyrénées. — *You can go skiing in the Pyrenees.*

Elle ne **pouvait** pas venir. — *She couldn't come.*

Il **a pu** manquer le train. — *He may have missed the train.*

Il **aurait pu** nous téléphoner. — *He could have phoned us.*

26.5 | *vouloir* ('to want', 'wish')

Je **voudrais** prendre rendez-vous avec le docteur. — *I'd like to make an appointment with the doctor.*

Je **voudrais** un demi-kilo de bananes. — *I'd like half a kilo of bananas.*

Faites comme vous **voudrez**. — *Do whatever you like.*

Voulez-vous me passer le pain, s'il vous plaît. — *Would you mind passing the bread, please.*

J'**aurai voulu** voir ça. — *I would have liked to have seen that.*

26.6 | *devoir*

The verb **devoir** has three different uses:

i) **devoir** *to owe*

When it means 'to owe', **devoir** is not followed by an infinitive:

— Je te **dois** combien? — *How much do I owe you?*
— Tu me **dois** 20 francs. — *You owe me 20 francs.*

ii) **devoir** *to have to, must*

With this meaning, **devoir** is nearly always followed by the infinitive of a second verb:

Excuse-moi, je **dois me dépêcher**. — *Sorry, I have to rush off.*

Ça **doit être** sa sœur. — *That must be his sister.*

Vous **devez avoir** faim. — *You must be hungry.*

J'**ai dû travailler** tard. — *I had to work late.*

Il **devait être** minuit quand nous sommes rentrés. — *It must have been midnight when we got back.*

iii) **devoir** *ought to, should*

When used in the Conditional or Conditional Perfect tense, **devoir** means 'ought', 'should', 'ought to have':

Je **devrais** leur téléphoner.	*I ought to phone them.*
Tu **devrais** venir me voir en Angleterre, l'année prochaine.	*You ought to come and see me in England next year.*
Elle **devrait** venir.	*She should be coming.*
Vous **devriez** aller le voir.	*You ought to go and see him.*
J'**aurais dû** prendre l'avion.	*I should have travelled by plane.*
Tu **aurais dû** leur écrire.	*You should have written to them.*
Il **aurait dû** rentrer à minuit.	*He should have come home at midnight.*

26.7 Prefixes

Many verbs can be changed slightly by adding a **prefix** to the front of the verb, e.g. **re-** (or **ré-**), **dé** (or **dés-**) and **sur-**:

revenir	*to come back, return*
recharger	*to reload*
se déshabiller	*to undress*
décharger	*to unload*
survivre	*to survive, live on*
surcharger	*to overload*

26.8 *aller* + infinitive

The Present Tense of **aller** followed by the infinitive is a simple way of referring to events which will take place in the *fairly near future:*

Je **vais me coucher.**	*I'm going to bed.*
Tu **vas regarder** le film?	*Are you going to watch the film?*
Il **va manger.**	*He's going to eat.*
Nous **allons prendre** l'autobus.	*We're going to take the bus.*
Vous **allez jouer** au football?	*Are you going to play football?*
Ils **vont prendre** un verre.	*They're going to have a drink.*

The Imperfect Tense of **aller** followed by the infinitive is used to describe what was *about to take place* when something happened:

Elle **allait partir** quand il est arrivé.	*She was going to leave when he arrived.*

26.9 | *venir de* + infinitive

Venir de + the infinitive is used to say that something *has just happened:*

Je **viens de déjeuner.**	*I've just had lunch.*
Elle **vient de téléphoner.**	*She's just phoned.*

The Imperfect Tense is used to describe what *had just happened:*

Nous **venions d'arriver** en France quand nous avons perdu nos bagages.	*We had just arrived in France when we lost our luggage.*
Ils **venaient de partir** quand la police est arrivée.	*They had just left when the police arrived.*

26.10 | *depuis* and *ça fait ... que*

These expressions of time are used with the Present Tense when the action is *still going on:*

Je l'attends **depuis** deux heures.	*I've been waiting for him for two hours.* (and still am)
Depuis quand travailles-tu en France?	*For how long have you been working in France?*
Ça fait trois jours **que** je travaille ici.	*I've been working here for three days.*

Depuis can also be used with the Imperfect Tense to give the sense of *had been:*

Elle apprenait le piano **depuis** trois ans.	*She had been learning the piano for three years*

27 Verbs with similar meanings

27.1 | *savoir* and *connaître*

savoir	*to know (have knowledge of, know a fact)*
connaître	*to know (be familiar, acquainted with)*

Je ne **savais** pas que son père était mort.	*I didn't know that his father was dead.*
Je ne **connaissais** pas son père.	*I didn't know his father.*
Connaissez-vous bien Paris?	*Do you know Paris well?*

Saviez-vous que le Centre Pompidou est devenu un des monuments le plus populaire à Paris?	*Did you know that the Pompidou Centre has become one of the most popular sights in Paris?*
Je n'en **sais** rien.	*I don't know anything about it.*
Tu **connais** la route?	*Do you know the way?*

27.2 *savoir* and *pouvoir*

savoir *can (to know how to)*
pouvoir *can (to be able to, have permission to)*

Je ne **sais** pas faire du ski.	*I can't ski. (I don't know how...)*
Je ne **peux** pas faire du ski ce week-end.	*I can't go skiing this week-end. (I'm unable...)*
Il **sait** très bien taper à la machine.	*He can type very well.*
Il **peut** vous voir ce soir.	*He can see you this evening.*

27.3 *avoir mal* and *se faire mal*

avoir mal *to have a pain*
se faire mal *to hurt oneself*

— Tu **t'es fait mal?**	— *Have you hurt yourself?*
— Oui, je **me suis fait mal** au pied.	— *Yes, I've hurt my foot.*
— Qu'est-ce qui ne va pas?	— *What's wrong?*
— J'**ai mal** au dos et je ne peux pas dormir.	— *I've got backache and I can't sleep.*

27.4 *penser, penser à* and *penser de*

penser + infinitive *to think of doing something*
penser à *to think about (reflect on)*
penser de *to think of (have an opinion on)*

Je **pense** partir lundi.	*I'm thinking of leaving on Monday.*
À quoi **penses**-tu?	*What are you thinking about?*
Que **pensez**-vous **du** nouveau gouvernement?	*What do you think of the new government?*

Penser à also has the sense of 'not to forget to do something':

Pense à lui téléphoner, ce soir.

93

27.5 s'asseoir and être assis

s'asseoir *to sit down* (action)
être assis *to be seated* (state)

Asseyez-vous!   *Sit down!*
Nous **étions assis** par terre.   *We sat (were sitting) on the floor.*

27.6 jouer de and jouer à

jouer de   *to play (musical instruments)*
jouer à   *to play (sports and games)*

— Vous **jouez d'**un instrument de musique?
— Oui, je **joue de** la guitare et du violon et mon frère **joue du** piano.
— Tu **joues au** rugby?
— Non, mais je **joue au** football.
Dans le Pays basque on **joue à** la pelote.
Ma sœur aime **jouer aux** cartes.

Note: **Faire de** is used in the sense of practising a sport:

Je **fais de** l'athlétisme et de la natation.

27.7 Verbs of saying and speaking

i) **dire**   *to say*

Qu'est-ce qu'il **a dit?**   *What did he say?*
Tu lui **as dit** de venir ce soir, n'est-ce   *You told her to come this evening, didn*
pas?   *you?*
Dis-lui "Bonjour" de ma part.   *Say 'hello' to him for me.*
"Si ça continue comme ça, **dit**-il* à   *"If this continues" he said to Christine,*
Christine, on rentrera demain."   *"we'll go home tomorrow."*

ii) **demander**   *to ask*

"Quelle heure est-il?" a-t-elle demandé*.   *(... she asked)*
Je lui **ai demandé** de venir.   *I asked him to come.*
Il lui **a demandé** son numéro de téléphone.   *He asked her for her telephone number.*

* Notice that the subject and verb are inverted (turned round) after direct speech.

iii) **parler**   *to speak*

Est-ce que vous **parlez** anglais?	*Do you speak English?*
C'est à vous, que je **parlais** tout à l'heure?	*Was it you I was speaking to a moment ago?*
Il **parlait** à voix basse.	*He spoke in a low voice.*

iv) **raconter**   *to recount, tell about*

Racontez-moi tout ce que vous avez fait à Paris.	*Tell me all about what you did in Paris.*
Il leur **a raconté** une histoire.	*He told them a story.*
Dans ce livre, on **raconte** la vie du Général de Gaulle.	*This book tells you about the life of General de Gaulle.*

28 | Impersonal verbs

Some verbs are only used in the 3rd person singular. They are often used in the Present Tense, but can also be used in other tenses.

28.1 | *il faut* ('it is necessary', 'must', 'have to', 'need')

Il **faut** partir tout de suite.	*We must leave straight away.*
Il vous **faut** partir tout de suite.	*You must leave straight away.*
Il **faut** deux heures pour aller à Paris.	*It takes two hours to get to Paris.*
Il **faut** manger pour vivre.	*You must eat to live.*
J'ai tout ce qu'**il** me **faut**.	*I've got everything I need.*

Note: Il faut can also be used with the Subjunctive (*see* Section 34).

28.2 | *il y a* ('there is', 'there are')

À Lyon, **il y a** un métro.	
Il y a beaucoup à voir à Lyon.	
Quand j'étais là, **il y avait** la fête de Lyon.	*When I was there, the Lyon festival was on.*
Il y avait du monde dans la rue.	*There were a lot of people in the streets.*
Aujourd'hui, **il y a** du vent.	
Ce matin, **il y avait** du brouillard.	

Note: Il y a + time means 'ago'. (*See* 15.1 (ii))

28.3 | *il s'agit de* ('it's about', 'it consists of')

De quoi **s'agit-il?**   *What's it all about? What does it consist of?*

Il s'agit d'une nouvelle méthode   *It's about a new way of learning the piano.*
d'apprendre le piano.

28.4 | *il vaut mieux* ('it's better to')

Il vaut mieux prendre l'autoroute.   *It's better to take the motorway.*
Il vaudrait mieux partir plus tôt.   *It would be better to leave earlier.*

28.5 | *ça vous plaît?* ('do you like it?')

This expression, which means literally 'does it please you?', is frequently used in
conversation in the Present and Perfect Tenses. Notice how it can be used with different
pronouns:

  — **Ça te plaît,** Paris?   — *Do you like Paris?*
  — Oui, **ça me plaît** beaucoup.   — *Yes, I like it very much.*
  — **Ça vous a plu,** la Tour Eiffel?   — *Did you like the Eiffel Tower?*
  — Oui, **ça m'a plu.**   — *Yes, I liked it.*

Note: This form of expression is also used with other verbs, in particular the following:

Ça m'intéresse beaucoup.   *I'm very interested in that.*
Le sport, **ça le passionne.**   *He's really enthusiastic about sport.*
Ça ne **te paraît** pas bizarre?   *Don't you think that's odd?*

28.6 | Weather expressions

il pleut   *it's raining*
il neige   *it's snowing*
il gèle   *it's freezing*

Il va pleuvoir.   *It's going to rain.*
Il neigeait tous les jours.   *It snowed every day.*
Il va geler ce soir.   *It'll freeze tonight.*

29   Verb constructions

In French it is common to find two verbs in a sentence: a main verb followed by an infinitive. Sometimes the infinitive follows directly, sometimes you must use **à** or **de** before the infinitive.

29.1   Verbs followed directly by the infinitive

aimer	*to like, love*
aller	*to go*
compter	*to count on*
désirer	*to want, wish*
devoir	*to have to, must*
entendre	*to hear*
espérer	*to hope*
faillir	*to nearly do something*
monter	*to go upstairs*
oser	*to dare*
penser	*to think of doing something*
pouvoir	*to be able, can*
préférer	*to prefer*
savoir	*to know (how to)*
venir	*to come*
voir	*to see*
vouloir	*to want, wish*

Elle **comptait** te **voir**.	*She was counting on seeing you.*
J'**espère venir** au mois d'août.	*I'm hoping to come in August.*
Ils **ont failli manquer** le train.	*They nearly missed the train.*
Il **est monté chercher** ses affaires.	*He went upstairs to look for his things.*
On n'**a** pas **osé parler**.	*We didn't dare speak.*
Tu **penses venir** à Londres, un de ces jours?	*Are you thinking of coming to London one of these days?*
Vous **êtes venu** exprès le **voir**?	*Did you come to see him on purpose?*

Notice how the verbs of 'seeing' and 'hearing' are used:

J'**ai entendu crier** quelqu'un .	*I heard someone shout.*
Puis, j'**ai vu** un homme **courir** vers le métro.	*Then I saw a man running towards the métro.*

29.2 Verbs followed by *à* + the infinitive

aider quelqu'un à	*to help someone*
apprendre à	*to learn*
chercher à	*to look for*
commencer à	*to begin*
consentir à	*to agree*
continuer à	*to continue*
se décider à	*to resolve*
hésiter à	*to hesitate*
s' intéresser à	*to be interested in*
inviter quelqu'un à	*to invite someone*
se mettre à	*to begin*
passer (du temps) à	*to spend time*
réussir à	*to succeed*

Je l'ai aidé à changer le pneu.	*I helped him change the tyre.*
Est-ce que tu apprends à taper à la machine?	*Are you learning to type?*
Il a commencé à pleuvoir.	*It began to rain.*
Elle s'est décidée à suivre un régime.	*She resolved to go on a diet.*
On a passé deux heures à trouver un hôtel.	*We spent two hours finding a hotel.*

29.3 Verbs followed by *de* + the infinitive

s' arrêter de	*to stop*
cesser de	*to cease, stop*
se dépêcher de	*to hurry*
décider de	*to decide*
essayer de	*to try*
finir de	*to finish*
menacer de	*to threaten*
être obligé de	*to be obliged, to have to*
oublier de	*to forget*
refuser de	*to refuse*
se souvenir de	*to remember*

Il **a cessé de neiger**.	*It's stopped snowing.*
Elle **a décidé de partir** plus tôt.	*She decided to leave ea.*
J'ai **fini de manger**.	*I've finished eating.*
Nous **étions obligés de rester** jusqu'au matin.	*We had to stay until the morning.*
Vous **avez refusé de** le **voir?**	*Did you refuse to see him?*

Note also the following expressions with **avoir** which are followed by **de** + the infinitive

avoir besoin de	*to need*
avoir l'intention de	*to intend*
avoir peur de	*to be afraid*
avoir le droit de	*to have the right*
avoir le temps de	*to have time to*
avoir envie de	*to wish*

Avez-vous **besoin de** regarder la carte?	*Do you need to look at the map?*
Elle **avait peur de** dire la vérité.	*She was afraid to tell the truth.*
Je n'ai pas **le temps de** le voir.	*I haven't got time to see him.*

29.4	Verbs followed by *à* + person + *de* + the infinitive

commander	*to order*
conseiller	*to advise*
défendre	*to forbid*
demander	*to ask*
dire	*to tell*
ordonner	*to order*
permettre	*to allow*
promettre	*to promise*
proposer	*to suggest*

J'ai **conseillé à** mes parents **de passer** deux jours à Rouen.	*I advised my parents to spend two days in Rouen.*
Elle **a demandé à** sa correspondante **d'envoyer** une photo.	*She asked her penfriend to send a photo.*
Il **permet à** sa fille **de conduire** sa voiture.	*He allows his daughter to drive his car.*

30   The infinitive

30.1   The infinitive after prepositions

The infinitive can be used after the following prepositions:

au lieu de	*instead of*	**pour**	*in order to*
avant de	*before*	**sans**	*without*

Avant de partir elle m'avait donné son adresse.
She gave me her address before she left.

Au lieu de rester au lit, il devrait se lever et faire sa valise.
Instead of staying in bed, he ought to get up and pack his case.

Il faut manger **pour vivre** et non pas vivre **pour manger**.
You should eat to live, not live to eat.

Ils sont partis **sans** nous **dire** ''au revoir''. *They left without saying goodbye to us.*

Note: See Section 31 for use of the past infinitive with **après** and Section 32 for the present participle used with **en**.

30.2   The infinitive in the negative

When the infinitive is in the negative, both parts of the negative go in front:

Elle m'a persuadé de **ne rien dire**.
She persuaded me not to say anything.

Je lui demanderai de **ne pas rentrer** trop tard.
I'll ask him not to come home too late.

31   'After doing' something (*après avoir* ... etc.)

In French, this phrase is translated by **après avoir** or **après être** + past participle:

Après avoir téléphoné au bureau, je suis parti.   *After phoning the office, I left.*

Après avoir visité la cathédrale, on est allés aux magasins.
We went to the shops after we'd visited the cathedral.

Après être arrivée à Paris, elle est allée directement à son hôtel.
After arriving in Paris, she went straight to her hotel.

Après s'être échappés, ils sont allés directement à la gare.
After escaping, they went straight to the station.

Après les **avoir vus** à la télé, on a décidé d'aller les voir en concert.	*After seeing them on TV, we decided to go and see them in concert.*

Note:
1. The same rules about the agreement of the past participle apply as in the Perfect Tense.
2. This structure can only be used when the subject is the same for both verbs.

32 *en* + present participle

32.1 Use of the present participle

En + **the present participle** is used when you want to describe two actions which happen more or less *at the same time:*

En sortant de l'hôtel, tournez à droite.	*Turn right when you go out of the hotel.*

It is also used to translate the English 'by -ing' or 'while -ing' when the subject is the same for both verbs (i.e. *We* took the taxi and *we* are bound to arrive in time; *He* broke his leg while *he* was skiing):

En prenant un taxi, on est sûr d'arriver à l'heure.	*By taking a taxi, we're bound to arrive in time.*
Il s'est cassé la jambe **en faisant** du ski.	*He broke his leg while skiing.*

Notice this special use of the present participle:

Il est sorti de la banque **en courant**.	*He ran out of the bank.*
Elle est entrée dans le bâtiment **en courant**.	*She ran into the building.*

32.2 How to form the present participle

The present participle is formed from the *nous* form of the verb.

The *-ons* ending is replaced by **-ant**:

Present Tense	*Present Participle*
nous sortons	**sortant**
nous prenons	**prenant**

Three important exceptions are:

avoir ⟶ **ayant**

être ⟶ **étant**

savoir ⟶ **sachant**

Ayant très peur, il a ouvert la porte.

Feeling very frightened, he opened the door.

Étant francophile, elle appréciera beaucoup ce livre.

Being a francophile (lover of France), she will really appreciate this book.

Sachant qu'il la trouverait chez sa mère, il y est allé tout de suite.

Knowing that he would find her at her mother's, he went there straight away.

33 The passive

The passive form of the verb is used when the subject, instead of *doing something* (active form), has something *done* to it:

He **saw** the girl.   (**Active**: *he* is doing the seeing)

He **was seen** by the girl. (**Passive**: he *is being seen*)

The passive is formed by using any tense of **être** with the past participle. The past participle is used like an adjective and agrees with the subject:

L'acteur américain **a été hospitalisé** ce matin.

The American actor was taken to hospital this morning.

Elle **a été renversée** par la voiture.

She was knocked down by the car.

La cathédrale **a été construite** au 16ème siècle.

The cathedral was built in the 16th century.

Avoiding the passive

If there is no mention of the person or thing who has performed the action, it is common in French to avoid using the passive by using the pronoun **on**:

On dit que ...

It is said that ...

On m'a averti que ...

I have been informed that ...

Sometimes, it is possible to avoid using the passive by using a reflexive verb:

Ça **se comprend**.

That's understood.

Ça ne **se traduit** pas (facilement).

That can't be translated (easily).

34 The Subjunctive

The Subjunctive is often used to express a *necessity,* a *wish,* a *fear,* a *possibility* or a *doubt,* or an *opinion.* It is also used after certain linking expressions and after the superlative. It is quite common in printed French and it is not difficult to understand as it often looks and sounds similar to the Present Tense.

34.1 Use of the Subjunctive

The verb in the Subjunctive is very rarely the main verb in the sentence. Often it is found in the part of the sentence introduced by *que:*

Il est normal qu'une fille **paye** sa part quand elle sort avec un garçon.

À mon avis, il est préférable que le garçon **paye** pour les deux.

i) It is used after the following phrases, to express an opinion (but not a certainty):

Il est préférable que ...	*It's better that ...*
Il est normal que ...	*It's right that ...*
Il est important que ...	*It's important that ...*
Il est dommage que ...	*It's a pity that ...*
Il vaut mieux que ...	*It's better that ...*
Pensez-vous que ...?	*Do you think that ...?*
Je ne crois pas que ...	*I don't think that ...*

Note: Verbs like **penser** and **croire** are usually only followed by the Subjunctive if they are in the negative or in question form. This suggests a *doubt* rather than a *certainty:*

Je ne pense pas qu'elle **puisse** venir.   *I don't think that she'll be able to come.*

Crois-tu qu'il **travaille** ce soir?   *Do you think he's working this evening?*

ii) The Subjunctive is used after expressions showing fear or emotion:

avoir peur que	*to be afraid that*
craindre que	*to be afraid that*
être content que	*to be happy that*
être étonné que	*to be amazed that*
regretter que	*to be sorry that*

J'**ai peur** qu'il ne **vienne** pas.   *I'm afraid that he won't come.*

Je **suis contente** qu'il **soit** là.   *I'm happy that he's there.*

iii) It is used to express doubt or uncertainty and to say that something is impossible:

douter que	*to doubt that*
Il est possible que...	*It's possible that...*
Il n'est pas certain que...	*It's unlikely that...*
Je ne suis pas sûr que ...	*I'm not sure that...*
Il est impossible que...	*It's impossible...*

Je **doute** qu'il **soit** là.	*I doubt that he's there.*
Il est possible que j'**aie** ton disque à la maison.	*It's possible that I've got your record at home.*
Je ne suis pas sûr que mes amis **puissent** nous accompagner.	*I'm not sure whether my friends will be able to come with us.*

iv) It is used to express a wish or preference to do something:

Je **veux** que tu m'**expliques** ça.	*I want you to explain that to me.*
Je **préfère** qu'il ne **vienne** pas.	*I'd rather that he didn't come.*

v) It is used to express a necessity or an obligation to do something:

Il est nécessaire que tu **partes**.	*You must leave.*
Il faut que vous leur **écriviez**.	*You must write to them.*

vi) The Subjunctive is used after the following words which link one part of the sentence to another:

afin que	*so that, in order that*
avant que...ne	*before*
bien que	*although*
jusqu'à ce que	*until*
à moins que ... ne	*unless*
pour que	*in order that*
pourvu que	*provided that*
quoique	*although*
sans que	*without*
de sorte que	*in such a way that*

J'ai bien aimé le film **quoique** je ne l'**aie** pas très bien compris.	*I really liked the film, although I didn't understand it very well.*
Donc, tu partiras mercredi, **à moins que** tes parents ne **partent** mardi.	*So, you'll be leaving on Wednesday, unless your parents leave on Tuesday.*

vii) It is used after **premier, dernier, seul** and **unique**:

Elle est la **seule** personne qui **sache** le faire.	*She is the only person who knows how to do it.*

viii) Finally, it is used after a superlative (i.e. 'the best', 'the greatest', 'the least', 'the smallest' etc.):

C'est la **meilleure** chose qui **puisse** arriver.

It's the best thing that could have happened.

C'est l'homme **le plus intelligent** que j'**aie** jamais connu.

He's the most intelligent man that I've ever known.

34.2 | How to form the Subjunctive

i) The Present Subjunctive of most verbs is easy to form. Start with the *ils/elles* form of the Present Tense:

ils ⎱
elles ⎰ **travaillent**

Take away the *ils/elles* and the *-ent* ending: **travaill**

This leaves the stem to which the endings below are added:

Subjunctive endings	-er *verb* travailler	-ir *verb* finir	-re *verb* attendre
-e -es -e	je **travaille** tu **travailles** il ⎫ elle ⎬ **travaille** on ⎭	je **finisse** tu **finisses** il ⎫ elle ⎬ **finisse** on ⎭	j' **attende** tu **attendes** il ⎫ elle ⎬ **attende** on ⎭
-ions -iez -ent	nous **travaillions** vous **travailliez** ils⎫ elles⎭**travaillent**	nous **finissions** vous **finissiez** ils⎫ elles⎭**finissent**	nous **attendions** vous **attendiez** ils⎫ elles⎭**attendent**

ii) The following verbs are irregular in the way that they form the Subjunctive. The *je* form of the Subjunctive is given here, but all parts of the verb are given in the verb table (pages 106-127):

aller   ⟶   j'**aille**   pouvoir ⟶ je **puisse**
avoir   ⟶   j'**aie**   savoir   ⟶ je **sache**
être   ⟶   je **sois**   vouloir ⟶ je **veuille**
faire   ⟶   je **fasse**

Regular verbs

Infinitive Present participle Imperative	Present	Perfect	Past Historic
jouer *to play* jouant joue! jouons! jouez!	je joue tu joues il joue nous jouons vous jouez ils jouent	j'ai joué tu as joué il a joué nous avons joué vous avez joué ils ont joué	je jouai tu jouas il joua nous jouâmes vous jouâtes ils jouèrent
attendre *to wait (for)* attendant attends! attendons! attendez!	j'attends tu attends il attend nous attendons vous attendez ils attendent	j'ai attendu tu as attendu il a attendu nous avons attendu vous avez attendu ils ont attendu	j'attendis tu attendis il attendit nous attendîmes vous attendîtes ils attendirent
finir *to finish* finissant finis! finissons! finissez!	je finis tu finis il finit nous finissons vous finissez ils finissent	j'ai fini tu as fini il a fini nous avons fini vous avez fini ils ont fini	je finis tu finis il finit nous finîmes vous finîtes ils finirent
se laver *to wash oneself* se lavant lave-toi! lavons-nous! lavez-vous!	je me lave tu te laves il se lave nous nous lavons vous vous lavez ils se lavent	je me suis lavé(e) tu t'es lavé(e) il s'est lavé elle s'est lavée nous nous sommes lavé(e)s vous vous êtes lavé(e)(s) ils se sont lavés elles se sont lavées	je me lavai tu te lavas il se lava nous nous lavâmes vous vous lavâtes ils se lavèrent

Imperfect	Future	Conditional	Subjunctive
je jouais	je jouerai	je jouerais	je joue
tu jouais	tu joueras	tu jouerais	tu joues
il jouait	il jouera	il jouerait	il joue
nous jouions	nous jouerons	nous jouerions	nous jouions
vous jouiez	vous jouerez	vous joueriez	vous jouiez
ils jouaient	ils joueront	ils joueraient	ils jouent
j'attendais	j'attendrai	j'attendrais	j'attende
tu attendais	tu attendras	tu attendrais	tu attendes
il attendait	il attendra	il attendrait	il attende
nous attendions	nous attendrons	nous attendrions	nous attendions
vous attendiez	vous attendrez	vous attendriez	vous attendiez
ils attendaient	ils attendront	ils attendraient	ils attendent
je finissais	je finirai	je finirais	je finisse
tu finissais	tu finiras	tu finirais	tu finisses
il finissait	il finira	il finirait	il finisse
nous finissions	nous finirons	nous finirions	nous finissions
vous finissiez	vous finirez	vous finiriez	vous finissiez
ils finissaient	ils finiront	ils finiraient	ils finissent
je me lavais	je me laverai	je me laverais	je me lave
tu te lavais	tu te laveras	tu te laverais	tu te laves
il se lavait	il se lavera	il se laverait	il se lave
nous nous lavions	nous nous laverons	nous nous laverions	nous nous lavions
vous vous laviez	vous vous laverez	vous vous laveriez	vous vous laviez
ils se lavaient	ils se laveront	ils se laveraient	ils se lavent

-er verbs with stem changes

1. Verbs like **acheter, lever, mener, peser, se promener**

Present	Future	Conditional
j'achète tu achètes il achète nous achetons vous achetez ils achètent	j'achèterai *etc.*	j'achèterais *etc.*

2. Verbs like **espérer, considérer, s'inquiéter, répéter, préférer**

Present
j'espère tu espères il espère nous espérons vous espérez ils espèrent

3. Verbs like **appeler, jeter, se rappeler**

Present	Future	Conditional
j'appelle tu appelles il appelle nous appelons vous appelez ils appellent	j'appellerai *etc.*	j'appellerais

4. Verbs ending in -**yer**, like **payer, essayer, appuyer, ennuyer, employer, nettoyer**

Present	Future	Conditional
je paie tu paies il paie nous payons vous payez ils paient	je paierai	je paierais

5. Verbs ending in -**ger** like **manger, ranger, changer, échanger, loger, obliger, partager, nager**

Present	Imperfect	Past Historic
je mange tu manges il mange nous mangeons vous mangez ils mangent	je mangeais *etc.*	je mangeai *etc.*

6. Verbs ending in -**cer** like **commencer, avancer, lancer, menacer, prononcer, remplacer**

Present	Imperfect	Past Historic
je commence tu commences il commence nous commençons vous commencez ils commencent	je commençais	je commençai

Irregular verbs

Infinitive Present participle Imperative	Present	Perfect	Past Historic
aller *to go* allant va! allons! allez!	je vais tu vas il va nous allons vous allez ils vont	je suis allé(e) tu es allé(e) il est allé elle est allée nous sommes allé(e)s vous êtes allé(e)(s) ils sont allés elles sont allées	j'allai tu allas il alla nous allâmes vous allâtes ils allèrent
apprendre *to learn* see **prendre**			
s'asseoir *to sit down* s'asseyant assieds-toi! asseyons-nous! asseyez-vous!	je m'assieds tu t'assieds il s'assied nous nous asseyons vous vous asseyez ils s'asseyent	je me suis assis(e) tu t'es assis(e) il s'est assis elle s'est assise nous nous sommes assis(e)s vous vous êtes assis(e)(es) ils se sont assis elles se sont assises	je m'assis tu t'assis il s'assit nous nous assîmes vous vous assîtes ils s'assirent
avoir *to have* ayant aie! ayons! ayez!	j'ai tu as il a nous avons vous avez ils ont	j'ai eu tu as eu il a eu nous avons eu vous avez eu ils ont eu	j'eus tu eus il eut nous eûmes vous eûtes ils eurent
battre *to beat* battant bats! battons! battez!	je bats tu bats il bat nous battons vous battez ils battent	j'ai battu tu as battu il a battu nous avons battu vous avez battu ils ont battu	je battis tu battis il battit nous battîmes vous battîtes ils battirent

Imperfect	Future	Conditional	Subjunctive
j'allais	j'irai	j'irais	j'aille
tu allais	tu iras	tu irais	tu ailles
il allait	il ira	il irait	il aille
nous allions	nous irons	nous irions	nous allions
vous alliez	vous irez	vous iriez	vous alliez
ils allaient	ils iront	ils iraient	ils aillent
je m'asseyais	je m'assiérai	je m'assiérais	je m'asseye
tu t'asseyais	tu t'assiéras	tu t'assiérais	tu t'asseyes
il s'asseyait	il s'assiéra	il s'assiérait	il s'asseye
nous nous asseyions	nous nous assiérons	nous nous assiérions	nous nous asseyions
vous vous asseyiez	vous vous assiérez	vous vous assiériez	vous vous asseyiez
ils s'asseyaient	ils s'assiéront	ils s'assiéraient	ils s'asseyent
j'avais	j'aurai	j'aureis	j'aie
tu avais	tu auras	tu aurais	tu aies
il avait	il aura	il aurait	il ait
nous avions	nous aurons	nous aurions	nous ayons
vous aviez	vous aurez	vous auriez	vous ayez
ils avaient	ils auront	ils auraient	ils aient
je battais	je battrai	je battrais	je batte
tu battais	tu battras	tu battrais	tu battes
il battait	il battra	il battrait	il batte
nous battions	nous battrons	nous battrions	nous battions
vous battiez	vous battrez	vous battriez	vous battiez
ils battaient	ils battront	ils battraient	ils battent

Infinitive Present participle Imperative	Present	Perfect	Past Historic
boire *to drink* buvant bois! buvons! buvez!	je bois tu bois il boit nous buvons vous buvez ils boivent	j'ai bu tu as bu il a bu nous avons bu vous avez bu ils ont bu	je bus tu bus il but nous bûmes vous bûtes ils burent

comprendre *to understand*   see **prendre**

conduire *to drive* conduisant conduis! conduisons! conduisez!	je conduis tu conduis il conduit nous conduisons vous conduisez ils conduisent	j'ai conduit tu as conduit il a conduit nous avons conduit vous avez conduit ils ont conduit	je conduisis tu conduisis il conduisit nous conduisîmes vous conduisîtes ils conduisirent
connaître *to know* connaissant connais! connaissons! connaissez!	je connais tu connais il connaît nous connaissons vous connaissez ils connaissent	j'ai connu tu as connu il a connu nous avons connu vous avez connu ils ont connu	je connus tu connus il connut nous connûmes vous connûtes ils connurent

construire *to build, construct*   see **conduire**

coudre *to sew* cousant couds! cousons! cousez!	je couds tu couds il coud nous cousons vous cousez ils cousent	j'ai cousu tu as cousu il a cousu nous avons cousu vous avez cousu ils ont cousu	je cousis tu cousis il cousit nous cousîmes vous cousîtes ils cousirent

Imperfect	Future	Conditional	Subjunctive
je buvais	je boirai	je boirais	je boive
tu buvais	tu boiras	tu boirais	tu boives
il buvait	il boira	il boirait	il boive
nous buvions	nous boirons	nous boirions	nous buvions
vous buviez	vous boirez	vous boiriez	vous buviez
ils buvaient	ils boiront	ils boiraient	ils boivent
je conduisais	je conduirai	je conduirais	je conduise
tu conduisais	tu conduiras	tu conduirais	tu conduises
il conduisait	il conduira	il conduirait	il conduise
nous conduisions	nous conduirons	nous conduirions	nous conduisions
vous conduisiez	vous conduirez	vous conduiriez	vous conduisiez
ils conduisaient	ils conduiront	ils conduiraient	ils conduisent
je connaissais	je connaîtrai	je connaîtrais	je connaisse
tu connaissais	tu connaîtras	tu connaîtrais	tu connaisses
il connaissait	il connaîtra	il connaîtrait	il connaisse
nous connaissions	nous connaîtrons	nous connaîtrions	nous connaissions
vous connaissiez	vous connaîtrez	vous connaîtriez	vous connaissiez
ils connaissaient	ils connaîtront	ils connaîtraient	ils connaissent
je cousais	je coudrai	je coudrais	je couse
tu cousais	tu coudras	tu coudrais	tu couses
il cousait	il coudra	il coudrait	il couse
nous cousions	nous coudrons	nous coudrions	nous cousions
vous cousiez	vous coudrez	vous coudriez	vous cousiez
ils cousaient	ils coudront	ils coudraient	ils cousent

Infinitive Present participle Imperative	Present	Perfect	Past Historic
courir *to run* courant cours! courons! courez!	je cours tu cours il court nous courons vous courez ils courent	j'ai couru tu as couru il a couru nous avons couru vous avez couru ils ont couru	je courus tu courus il courut nous courûmes vous courûtes ils coururent
craindre *to fear* craignant crains! craignons! craignez!	je crains tu crains il craint nous craignons vous craignez ils craignent	j'ai craint tu as craint il a craint nous avons craint vous avez craint ils ont craint	je craignis tu craignis il craignit nous craignîmes vous craignîtes ils craignirent
croire *to believe* croyant crois! croyons! croyez!	je crois tu crois il croit nous croyons vous croyez ils croient	j'ai cru tu as cru il a cru nous avons cru vous avez cru ils ont cru	je crus tu crus il crut nous crûmes vous crûtes ils crurent

découvrir *to discover*   see **ouvrir**

descendre *to go down* descendant descends! descendons! descendez!	je descends tu descends il descend nous descendons vous descendez ils descendent	je suis descendu(e) tu es descendu(e) il est descendu elle est descendue nous sommes descendu(e)s vous êtes descendu(e)(s) ils sont descendus elles sont descendues	je descendis tu descendis il descendit nous descendîmes vous descendîtes ils descendirent

devenir *to become*   see **venir**

Imperfect	Future	Conditional	Subjunctive
je courais	je courrai	je courrais	je coure
tu courais	tu courras	tu courrais	tu coures
il courait	il courra	il courrait	il coure
nous courions	nous courrons	nous courrions	nous courions
vous couriez	vous courrez	vous courriez	vous couriez
ils couraient	ils courront	ils courraient	ils courent
je craignais	je craindrai	je craindrais	je craigne
tu craignais	tu craindras	tu craindrais	tu craignes
il craignait	il craindra	il craindrait	il craigne
nous craignions	nous craindrons	nous craindrions	nous craignions
vous craigniez	vous craindrez	vous craindriez	vous craigniez
ils craignaient	ils craindront	ils craindraient	ils craignent
je croyais	je croirai	je croirais	je croie
tu croyais	tu croiras	tu croirais	tu croies
il croyait	il croira	il croirait	il croie
nous croyions	nous croirons	nous croirions	nous croyions
vous croyiez	vous croirez	vous croiriez	vous croyiez
ils croyaient	ils croiront	ils croiraient	ils croient
je descendais	je descendrai	je descendrais	je descende
tu descendais	tu descendras	tu descendrais	tu descendes
il descendait	il descendra	il descendrait	il descende
nous descendions	nous descendrons	nous descendrions	nous descendions
vous descendiez	vous descendrez	vous descendriez	vous descendiez
ils descendaient	ils descendront	ils descendraient	ils descendent

Infinitive Present participle Imperative	Present	Perfect	Past Historic
devoir *to have to, owe* devant dois! devons! devez!	je dois tu dois il doit nous devons vous devez ils doivent	j'ai dû tu as dû il a dû nous avons dû vous avez dû ils ont dû	je dus tu dus il dut nous dûmes vous dûtes ils durent
dire *to say* disant dis! disons! dites!	je dis tu dis il dit nous disons vous dites ils disent	j'ai dit tu as dit il a dit nous avons dit vous avez dit ils ont dit	je dis tu dis il dit nous dîmes vous dîtes ils dirent
dormir *to sleep* dormant dors! dormons! dormez!	je dors tu dors il dort nous dormons vous dormez ils dorment	j'ai dormi tu as dormi il a dormi nous avons dormi vous avez dormi ils ont dormi	je dormis tu dormis il dormit nous dormîmes vous dormîtes ils dormirent
écrire *to write* écrivant écris! écrivons! écrivez!	j'écris tu écris il écrit nous écrivons vous écrivez ils écrivent	j'ai écrit tu as écrit il a écrit nous avons écrit vous avez écrit ils ont écrit	j'écrivis tu écrivis il écrivit nous écrivîmes vous écrivîtes ils écrivirent
entendre *to hear* entendant entends! entendons! entendez!	j'entends tu entends il entend nous entendons vous entendez ils entendent	j'ai entendu tu as entendu il a entendu nous avons entendu vous avez entendu ils ont entendu	j'entendis tu entendis il entendit nous entendîmes vous entendîtes ils entendirent

Imperfect	Future	Conditional	Subjunctive
je devais	je devrai	je devrais	je doive
tu devais	tu devras	tu devrais	tu doives
il devait	il devra	il devrait	il doive
nous devions	nous devrons	nous devrions	nous devions
vous deviez	vous devrez	vous devriez	vous deviez
ils devaient	ils devront	ils devraient	ils doivent
je disais	je dirai	je dirais	je dise
tu disais	tu diras	tu dirais	tu dises
il disait	il dira	il dirait	il dise
nous disions	nous dirons	nous dirions	nous disions
vous disiez	vous direz	vous diriez	vous disiez
ils disaient	ils diront	ils diraient	ils disent
je dormais	je dormirai	je dormirais	je dorme
tu dormais	tu dormiras	tu dormirais	tu dormes
il dormait	il dormira	il dormirait	il dorme
nous dormions	nous dormirons	nous dormirions	nous dormions
vous dormiez	vous dormirez	vous dormiriez	vous dormiez
ils dormaient	ils dormiront	ils dormiraient	ils dorment
j'écrivais	j'écrirai	j'écrirais	j'écrive
tu écrivais	tu écriras	tu écrirais	tu écrives
il écrivait	il écrira	il écrirait	il écrive
nous écrivions	nous écrirons	nous écririons	nous écrivions
vous écriviez	vous écrirez	vous écririez	vous écriviez
ils écrivaient	ils écriront	ils écriraient	ils écrivent
j'entendais	j'entendrai	j'entendrais	j'entende
tu entendais	tu entendras	tu entendrais	tu entendes
il entendait	il entendra	il entendrait	il entende
nous entendions	nous entendrons	nous entendrions	nous entendions
vous entendiez	vous entendrez	vous entendriez	vous entendiez
ils entendaient	ils entendront	ils entendraient	ils entendent

Infinitive Present participle Imperative	Present	Perfect	Past Historic
envoyer *to send* envoyant envoie! envoyons! envoyez!	j'envoie tu envoies il envoie nous envoyons vous envoyez ils envoient	j'ai envoyé tu as envoyé il a envoyé nous avons envoyé vous avez envoyé ils ont envoyé	j'envoyai tu envoyas il envoya nous envoyâmes vous envoyâtes ils envoyèrent
éteindre *to put out,* *switch off* éteignant éteins! éteignons! éteignez!	j'éteins tu éteins il éteint nous éteignons vous éteignez ils éteignent	j'ai éteint tu as éteint il a éteint nous avons éteint vous avez éteint ils ont éteint	j'éteignis tu éteignis il éteignit nous éteignîmes vous éteignîtes ils éteignirent
être *to be* étant sois! soyons! soyez!	je suis tu es il est nous sommes vous êtes ils sont	j'ai été tu as été il a été nous avons été vous avez été ils ont été	je fus tu fus il fut nous fûmes vous fûtes ils furent
faire *to do, make* faisant fais! faisons! faites!	je fais tu fais il fait nous faisons vous faites ils font	j'ai fait tu as fait il a fait nous avons fait vous avez fait ils ont fait	je fis tu fis il fit nous fîmes vous fîtes ils firent
falloir *must, is* *necessary*	il faut	il a fallu	il fallut
lire *to read* lisant lis! lisons! lisez!	je lis tu lis il lit nous lisons vous lisez ils lisent	j'ai lu tu as lu il a lu nous avons lu vous avez lu ils ont lu	je lus tu lus il lut nous lûmes vous lûtes ils lurent

Imperfect	Future	Conditional	Subjunctive
j'envoyais	j'enverrai	j'enverrais	j'envoie
tu envoyais	tu enverras	tu enverrais	tu envoies
il envoyait	il enverra	il enverrait	il envoie
nous envoyions	nous enverrons	nous enverrions	nous envoyions
vous envoyiez	vous enverrez	vous enverriez	vous envoyiez
ils envoyaient	ils enverront	ils enverraient	ils envoient
j'éteignais	j'éteindrai	j'éteindrais	j'éteigne
tu éteignais	tu éteindras	tu éteindrais	tu éteignes
il éteignait	il éteindra	il éteindrait	il éteigne
nous éteignions	nous éteindrons	nous éteindrions	nous éteignions
vous éteigniez	vous éteindrez	vous éteindriez	vous éteigniez
ils éteignaient	ils éteindront	ils éteindraient	ils éteignent
j'étais	je serai	je serais	je sois
tu étais	tu seras	tu serais	tu sois
il était	il sera	il serait	il soit
nous étions	nous serons	nous serions	nous soyons
vous étiez	vous serez	vous seriez	vous soyez
ils étaient	ils seront	ils seraient ·	ils soient
je faisais	je ferai	je ferais	je fasse
tu faisais	tu feras	tu ferais	tu fasses
il faisait	il fera	il ferait	il fasse
nous faisions	nous ferons	nous ferions	nous fassions
vous faisiez	vous ferez	vous feriez	vous fassiez
ils faisaient	ils feront	ils feraient	ils fassent
il fallait	il faudra	il faudrait	il faille
je lisais	je lirai	je lirais	je lise
tu lisais	tu liras	tu lirais	tu lises
il lisait	il lira	il lirait	il lise
nous lisions	nous lirons	nous lirions	nous lisions
vous lisiez	vous lirez	vous liriez	vous lisiez
ils lisaient	ils liront	ils liraient	ils lisent

Infinitive Present participle Imperative	Present	Perfect	Past Historic
mettre *to put (on)* mettant mets! mettons! mettez!	je mets tu mets il met nous mettons vous mettez ils mettent	j'ai mis tu as mis il a mis nous avons mis vous avez mis ils ont mis	je mis tu mis il mit nous mîmes vous mîtes ils mirent
mourir *to die* mourant meurs! mourons! mourez!	je meurs tu meurs il meurt nous mourons vous mourez ils meurent	je suis mort(e) tu es mort(e) il est mort elle est morte nous sommes mort(e)s vous êtes mort(e)(s) ils sont morts elles sont mortes	je mourus tu mourus il mourut nous mourûmes vous mourûtes ils moururent
naître *to be born* naissant	je nais tu nais il naît nous naissons vous naissez ils naissent	je suis né(e) tu es né(e) il est né elle est née nous sommes né(e)s vous êtes né(e)(s) ils sont nés elles sont nées	je naquis tu naquis il naquit nous naquîmes vous naquîtes ils naquirent
offrir *to offer, give* see **ouvrir**			
ouvrir *to open* ouvrant ouvre! ouvrons! ouvrez!	j'ouvre tu ouvres il ouvre nous ouvrons vous ouvrez ils ouvrent	j'ai ouvert tu as ouvert il a ouvert nous avons ouvert vous avez ouvert ils ont ouvert	j'ouvris tu ouvris il ouvrit nous ouvrîmes vous ouvrîtes ils ouvrirent

Imperfect	Future	Conditional	Subjunctive
je mettais	je mettrai	je mettrais	je mette
tu mettais	tu mettras	tu mettrais	tu mettes
il mettait	il mettra	il mettrait	il mette
nous mettions	nous mettrons	nous mettrions	nous mettions
vous mettiez	vous mettrez	vous mettriez	vous mettiez
ils mettaient	ils mettront	ils mettraient	ils mettent
je mourais	je mourrai	je mourrais	je meure
tu mourais	tu mourras	tu mourrais	tu meures
il mourait	il mourra	il mourrait	il meure
nous mourions	nous mourrons	nous mourrions	nous mourions
vous mouriez	vous mourrez	vous mourriez	vous mouriez
ils mouraient	ils mourront	ils mourraient	ils meurent
je naissais	je naîtrai	je naîtrais	je naisse
tu naissais	tu naîtras	tu naîtrais	tu naisses
il naissait	il naîtra	il naîtrait	il naisse
nous naissions	nous naîtrons	nous naîtrions	nous naissions
vous naissiez	vous naîtrez	vous naîtriez	vous naissiez
ils naissaient	ils naîtront	ils naîtraient	ils naissent
j'ouvrais	j'ouvrirai	j'ouvrirais	j'ouvre
tu ouvrais	tu ouvriras	tu ouvrirais	tu ouvres
il ouvrait	il ouvrira	il ouvrirait	il ouvre
nous ouvrions	nous ouvrirons	nous ouvririons	nous ouvrions
vous ouvriez	vous ouvrirez	vous ouvririez	vous ouvriez
ils ouvraient	ils ouvriront	ils ouvriraient	ils ouvrent

Infinitive Present participle Imperative	Present	Perfect	Past Historic
paraître *to appear* see **connaître**			
partir *to leave* partant pars! partons! partez!	je pars tu pars il part nous partons vous partez ils partent	je suis parti(e) tu es parti(e) il est parti elle est partie nous sommes parti(e)s vous êtes parti(e)(s) ils sont partis elles sont parties	je partis tu partis il partit nous partîmes vous partîtes ils partirent
pleuvoir *to rain* pleuvant	il pleut	il a plu	il plut
pouvoir *to be able, can*	je peux tu peux il peut nous pouvons vous pouvez ils peuvent	j'ai pu tu as pu il a pu nous avons pu vous avez pu ils ont pu	je pus tu pus il put nous pûmes vous pûtes ils purent
prendre *to take* prenant prends! prenons! prenez!	je prends tu prends il prend nous prenons vous prenez ils prennent	j'ai pris tu as pris il a pris nous avons pris vous avez pris ils ont pris	je pris tu pris il prit nous prîmes vous prîtes ils prirent
recevoir *to receive* recevant reçois! recevons! recevez!	je reçois tu reçois il reçoit nous recevons vous recevez ils reçoivent	j'ai reçu tu as reçu il a reçu nous avons reçu vous avez reçu ils ont reçu	je reçus tu reçus il reçut nous reçûmes vous reçûtes ils reçurent

Imperfect	Future	Conditional	Subjunctive
je partais	je partirai	je partirais	je parte
tu partais	tu partiras	tu partirais	tu partes
il partait	il partira	il partirait	il parte
nous partions	nous partirons	nous partirions	nous partions
vous partiez	vous partirez	vous partiriez	vous partiez
ils partaient	ils partiront	ils partiraient	ils partent
il pleuvait	il pleuvra	il pleuvrait	il pleuve
je pouvais	je pourrai	je pourrais	je puisse
tu pouvais	tu pourras	tu pourrais	tu puisses
il pouvait	il pourra	il pourrait	il puisse
nous pouvions	nous pourrons	nous pourrions	nous puissions
vous pouviez	vous pourrez	vous pourriez	vous puissiez
ils pouvaient	ils pourront	ils pourraient	ils puissent
je prenais	je prendrai	je prendrais	je prenne
tu prenais	tu prendras	tu prendrais	tu prennes
il prenait	il prendra	il prendrait	il prenne
nous prenions	nous prendrons	nous prendrions	nous prenions
vous preniez	vous prendrez	vous prendriez	vous preniez
ils prenaient	ils prendront	ils prendraient	ils prennent
je recevais	je recevrai	je recevrais	je reçoive
tu recevais	tu recevras	tu recevrais	tu reçoives
il recevait	il recevra	il recevrait	il reçoive
nous recevions	nous recevrons	nous recevrions	nous recevions
vous receviez	vous recevrez	vous recevriez	vous receviez
ils recevaient	ils recevront	ils recevraient	ils reçoivent

Infinitive Present participle Imperative	Present	Perfect	Past Historic
reconnaître *to recognise* see **connaître**			
revenir *to come back, return* see **venir**			
rire *to laugh* riant ris! rions! riez!	je ris tu ris il rit nous rions vous riez ils rient	j'ai ri tu as ri il a ri nous avons ri vous avez ri ils ont ri	je ris tu ris il rit nous rîmes vous rîtes ils rirent
savoir *to know* sachant sache! sachons! sachez!	je sais tu sais il sait nous savons vous savez ils savent	j'ai su tu as su il a su nous avons su vous avez su ils ont su	je sus tu sus il sut nous sûmes vous sûtes ils surent
sortir *to go out* see **partir**			
suivre *to follow* suivant suis! suivons! suivez!	je suis tu suis il suit nous suivons vous suivez ils suivent	j'ai suivi tu as suivi il a suivi nous avons suivi vous avez suivi ils ont suivi	je suivis tu suivis il suivit nous suivîmes vous suivîtes ils suivirent
tenir *to hold* see **venir**			
venir *to come* venant viens! venons! venez!	je viens tu viens il vient nous venons vous venez ils viennent	je suis venu(e) tu es venu(e) il est venu elle est venue nous sommes venu(e)s vous êtes venu(e)(s) ils sont venus elles sont venues	je vins tu vins il vint nous vînmes vous vîntes ils vinrent

Imperfect	Future	Conditional	Subjunctive
je riais	je rirai	je rirais	je rie
tu riais	tu riras	tu rirais	tu ries
il riait	il rira	il rirait	il rie
nous riions	nous rirons	nous ririons	nous riions
vous riiez	vous rirez	vous ririez	vous riiez
ils riaient	ils riront	ils riraient	ils rient
je savais	je saurai	je saurais	je sache
tu savais	tu sauras	tu saurais	tu saches
il savait	il saura	il saurait	il sache
nous savions	nous saurons	nous saurions	nous sachions
vous saviez	vous saurez	vous sauriez	vous sachiez
ils savaient	ils sauront	ils sauraient	ils sachent
je suivais	je suivrai	je suivrais	je suive
tu suivais	tu suivras	tu suivrais	tu suives
il suivait	il suivra	il suivrait	il suive
nous suivions	nous suivrons	nous suivrions	nous suivions
vous suiviez	vous suivrez	vous suivriez	vous suiviez
ils suivaient	ils suivront	ils suivraient	ils suivent
je venais	je viendrai	je viendrais	je vienne
tu venais	tu viendras	tu viendrais	tu viennes
il venait	il viendra	il viendrait	il vienne
nous venions	nous viendrons	nous viendrions	nous venions
vous veniez	vous viendrez	vous viendriez	vous veniez
ils venaient	ils viendront	ils viendraient	ils viennent

Infinitive Present participle Imperative	Present	Perfect	Past Historic
vivre *to live* vivant vis! vivons! vivez!	je vis tu vis il vit nous vivons vous vivez ils vivent	j'ai vécu tu as vécu il a vécu nous avons vécu vous avez vécu ils ont vécu	je vécus tu vécus il vécut nous vécûmes vous vécûtes ils vécurent
voir *to see* voyant vois! voyons! voyez!	je vois tu vois il voit nous voyons vous voyez ils voient	j'ai vu tu as vu il a vu nous avons vu vous avez vu ils ont vu	je vis tu vis il vit nous vîmes vous vîtes ils virent
vouloir *to want, wish* voulant veuille! veuillons! veuillez!	je veux tu veux il veut nous voulons vous voulez ils veulent	j'ai voulu tu as voulu il a voulu nous avons voulu vous avez voulu ils ont voulu	je voulus tu voulus il voulut nous voulûmes vous voulûtes ils voulurent

Imperfect	Future	Conditional	Subjunctive
je vivais	je vivrai	je vivrais	je vive
tu vivais	tu vivras	tu vivrais	tu vives
il vivait	il vivra	il vivrait	il vive
nous vivions	nous vivrons	nous vivrions	nous vivions
vous viviez	vous vivrez	vous vivriez	vous viviez
ils vivaient	ils vivront	ils vivraient	ils vivent
je voyais	je verrai	je verrais	je voie
tu voyais	tu verras	tu verrais	tu voies
il voyait	il verra	il verrait	il voie
nous voyions	nous verrons	nous verrions	nous voyions
vous voyiez	vous verrez	vous verriez	vous voyiez
ils voyaient	ils verront	ils verraient	ils voient
je voulais	je voudrai	je voudrais	je veuille
tu voulais	tu voudras	tu voudrais	tu veuilles
il voulait	il voudra	il voudrait	il veuille
nous voulions	nous voudrons	nous voudrions	nous voulions
vous vouliez	vous voudrez	vous voudriez	vous vouliez
ils voulaient	ils voudront	ils voudraient	ils veuillent

1 You, your family and pets

une adresse	address	habiter	to live
un(e) adulte	adult	un hamster	hamster
âge	age	un homme	man
âgé: plus (moins)..	older (younger)	jeune	young
aîné	older	un lapin	rabbit
un(e) ami(e)	friend	maman	mum
anglais	English	le mari	husband
un animal	animal	le mariage	wedding
l' anniversaire (m)	birthday	une mère	mother
un aquarium	aquarium	mort(e)	dead
l' argent de poche (m)	pocket money	la nationalité	nationality
		né	born
un beau-frère	brother-in-law	un neveu	nephew
les beaux-parents (m.pl.)	parents-in-law	une nièce	niece
		le nom	name
une belle-sœur	sister-in-law	le numéro de téléphone	telephone number
un bébé	baby		
le cadet (la cadette)	the youngest	l' oiseau (m)	bird
une cage	cage	un oncle	uncle
un(e) camarade	friend	papa	dad
catholique	Catholic	un parent	relation, parent
célibataire	single	une patte	paw
un chat (une chatte)	cat	un père	father
un cheval	horse	un perroquet	parrot
un chien (une chienne)	dog	une perruche	budgerigar
		un(e) petit(e) ami(e)	boyfriend (girlfriend)
un cochon d'Inde	guinea pig	les petits enfants (m.pl.)	grandchildren
un copain (une copine)	friend		
		un poisson (rouge)	(gold)fish
un(e) cousin(e)	cousin	le prénom	Christian name
divorcé	divorced	se présenter	to introduce yourself
un(e) enfant	child		
un étranger	foreigner	protestant	Protestant
une famille	family	la queue	tail
une femme	wife, woman	un singe	monkey
un(e) fiancé(e)	fiancé(e)	une sœur	sister
une fille	daughter, girl	une souris	mouse
un fils	son	une tante	aunt
un frère	brother	une tortue	tortoise
un garçon	boy	unique	only
une grand-mère	grandmother	un veuf (une veuve)	widower (widow)
un grand-père	grandfather	vieux	old
les grands-parents (m.pl)	grandparents	un voisin	neighbour

2 | In the home

allumer	to switch on	un garage	garage
un appartement	flat	le gaz	gas
une armoire	wardrobe	un grenier	attic
un ascenseur	lift	un jardin	garden
un aspirateur	vacuum cleaner	une lampe	lamp
une assiette	plate	un lavabo	wash-basin
une baignoire	bath	un lave-vaisselle	dishwasher
un balcon	balcony	un lit	bed
une bibliothèque	bookcase	la lumière	light
un bol	bowl	une machine à	sewing machine
un bouchon	cork	coudre	
brancher	to plug in	une machine à laver	washing machine
un buffet	sideboard	un magnétophone	tape recorder
la campagne	countryside	un magnétoscope	video recorder
un canapé	sofa	les meubles (m.pl.)	furniture
une casserole	saucepan	un micro-ordinateur	micro-computer
une cave	cellar	le mur	wall
une chaise	chair	une nappe	tablecloth
une chambre	bedroom	le palier	landing
le chauffage central	central heating	un panier	basket
une cheminée	chimney	un pavillon	detached house
un cintre	coat-hanger	une pelouse	lawn
des ciseaux (m.pl.)	scissors	une pendule	clock
une clé	key	une pièce	room
une commode	chest of drawers	un placard	cupboard
un congélateur	deep-freeze	le plafond	ceiling
un couteau	knife	le plancher	floor
une couverture	blanket	une poêle	frying pan
une cuillère	spoon	une porte	door
une cuisine	kitchen	une poubelle	dustbin
une cuisinière	cooker	un propriétaire	owner
une douche	shower	une prise de courant	electric point
des draps (m.pl.)	sheets	un radiateur	radiator
une échelle	ladder	un rayon	shelf
un électrophone	record player	un réveille-matin	alarm clock
un escalier	staircase	le rez-de-chaussée	ground floor
éteindre	to switch off	un rideau	curtain
un évier	sink	un robinet	tap
un fauteuil	armchair	une salle	room
un fer à repasser	iron	une salle à manger	dining room
un feu	fire	une salle de bains	bathroom
un four	stove	une salle de séjour	living room
une fourchette	fork	un salon	lounge
un réfrigérateur	fridge		

une serviette	towel	une tasse	cup
un studio	bed-sitter	un téléviseur	TV set
le sous-sol	basement	la toilette	toilet
une table	table	le toit	roof
un tableau	picture	un torchon	tea-towel
un tablier	apron	un verre	glass
un tapis	carpet		

3 | In town

un arrêt d'autobus	bus stop	un hôpital	hospital
une avenue	street, avenue	un hôtel de ville	town hall
la banlieue	suburb	un immeuble	block of flats
une banque	bank	un jardin public	public gardens
un bâtiment	building	un lycée	secondary school
une bibliothèque	library	une mairie	town hall
le boulevard périphérique	ring road	une maison de la culture	arts centre or theatre
une boutique	small shop	un marché	market
un bureau (de change)	(foreign exchange) office	marché: la place du ...	market square
un café	café	un monument	building of historical interest
un carrefour	crossroads		
une cathédrale	cathedral		
le centre commercial	shopping precinct	municipal	owned by the Council
le centre-ville	town centre	un musée	museum
un château	castle	un office de tourisme	tourist office
un cinéma	cinema		
un coin	corner	un panneau	sign, road sign
le commissariat de police	police station	un parking	car-park
		un passage à niveau	level-crossing
une église	church	un passage souterrain	subway
les feux (rouges, verts) (m.pl.)	traffic lights	un piéton	pedestrian
la gare	station	piétonne: une voie (une rue)...	pedestrian precinct
la gare routière	coach station	une piscine	swimming pool
la gendarmerie	police station	une place	square
un grand magasin	department store	le pont	bridge
une H.L.M.	'fixed-rent property' (equivalent to Council property)	le port	port
		la poste	post office
		un poteau	post

un prison	prison	un syndicat	tourist office
un quartier	district; area	d'initiative	
un restaurant	restaurant	un terrain de sports	sports ground
un rond-point	roundabout	un théâtre	theatre
une route	road	une tour	tower
une rue	street	le trottoir	pavement
un stade	stadium	une université	university
une station de métro	métro station	une usine	factory
une station-service	garage selling petrol		
un supermarché	supermarket	For full list of shops, see page 144.

---

4 | In the country

un agneau	lamb	un mouton	sheep
agricole	agricultural	la nature	nature
un arbre	tree	un oiseau	bird
un berger	shepherd	un ouvrier agricole	farm worker
un bois	wood	un parc régional naturel	regional park
le bord	edge	le paysage	countryside
une branche	branch	un paysan	small holder,
un buisson	bush		peasant
un camping	campsite	la pêche	fishing
un canard	duck	la plage	beach
un champ	field	une plante	plant
une colline	hill	en plein air	in the open air
une ferme	farm	une poule	hen
un fermier	farmer	une prairie	meadow
une feuille	leaf	une randonnée	ramble, hike
une fleur	flower	un renard	fox
un fleuve	river	une rivière	river
la forêt	forest	un rocher	rock
un fruit	fruit	sauvage	wild
la haie	hedge	un sentier	path
l' herbe (f)	grass	un serpent	snake
un insecte	insect	une vache	cow
un lac	lake	les vendanges (f.pl.)	grape harvest
un légume	vegetable	un verger	orchard
un lièvre	hare	un vignoble	vineyard
la lune	moon	un village	village
la mer	sea		
une montagne	mountain		

5 | Daily routine and household chores

se réveiller	to wake up
se lever	to get up
se laver	to get washed
s'habiller	to get dressed
prendre son petit déjeuner	to have breakfast
aller à l'école (au travail)	to go to school (to work)
déjeuner	to have lunch
goûter	to have afternoon tea
rentrer	to return home
se déshabiller	to get undressed
prendre un bain (une douche)	to take a bath (a shower)
se coucher	to go to bed
dormir	to sleep

Mealtimes

le petit déjeuner	breakfast
le déjeuner	lunch
le goûter	tea
le dîner	dinner

Household chores

aider à la maison	to help at home
débarrasser la table	to clear the table
essuyer	to wipe up
faire les courses	to go shopping
faire la cuisine	to cook
faire les lits	to make the beds
faire le ménage	to do the housework
faire du repassage	to do the ironing
faire la vaisselle	to do the washing up
laver la voiture	to wash the car
mettre la table	to lay the table
nettoyer	to clean
passer l'aspirateur	to hoover
préparer les repas	to prepare the meals
ranger ses affaires	to tidy up
repasser	to iron
travailler dans le jardin	to work in the garden

anglais	English	un emploi du temps	timetable
apprendre	to learn	ennuyeux	boring
les arts ménagers	domestic science	l' espagnol (m)	Spanish
(m.pl.)		l' étude (f)	study period
un atelier	workshop	études: faire	to study
le bac (= le	equivalent to	des ...	
baccalauréat)	A-level	un étudiant	student
	examination	un examen	examination
un bic	biro	un exercice	exercise
la biologie	biology	facile	easy
un cahier	exercise book	facultatif (-ve)	optional
une calculatrice	calculator	faible	weak
un(e) camarade	class mate	une faute	fault
la cantine	dining hall	une feuille	sheet of paper
un carnet	notebook, pupil's	une fiche	note
	record book	fort (en)	strong, good
la chimie	chemistry		(at something)
la classe	class	le français	French
un collège	school for 11-16	la géographie	geography
	year olds	une gomme	rubber
le (la) concierge	caretaker	le gymnase	gymnasium
le couloir	corridor	l' histoire (f)	history
la cour	schoolyard	l' informatique (f)	computer studies
un cours	lesson	un(e) instituteur	primary school
la couture	sewing	(institutrice)	teacher
la craie	chalk	l' instruction	current affairs
un crayon	pencil	civique (f)	
la dactylo	typing	l' instruction	religious
un demi-	pupil who has	religieuse (f)	education
pensionnaire	lunch at school	intéressant	interesting
le dessin	(industrial)	un(e) interne	boarder
(industriel)	drawing	un jour	day
les devoirs (m.pl.)	homework	un jour de congé	a day's holiday
difficile	difficult	un laboratoire	(language)
le directeur (la	headmaster	(de langues)	laboratory
directrice)	(headmistress)	une langue étrangère	foreign language
échouer à un	to fail an	une langue vivante	modern language
examen	examination	une leçon	lesson
une école (primaire)	(primary) school	libre	free
l' éducation	(physical)	un livre	book
(physique) (m)	education	un lycée	school for 16-19
un(e) élève	pupil		year olds

un magnétophone	*tape recorder*
les mathématiques *(f.pl.)*	*maths*
une matière	*subject*
un micro-ordinateur	*micro-computer*
moyen	*average*
la musique	*music*
une note	*mark*
le niveau	*level*
obligatoire	*compulsory*
une page	*page*
le papier	*paper*
passer un examen	*to take an exam*
la physique	*physics*
un professeur	*teacher*
du progrès	*progress*
la récréation	*break*
reçu: être...	*to pass an examination*
la rentrée (scolaire)	*return to school*
une retenue	*detention*
une salle de classe	*classroom*
la salle des profs	*staffroom*
les sciences *(f.pl.)*	*science*
secondaire	*secondary*
la secrétaire	*secretary*
la sonnerie	*bell*
un stylo	*pen*
un surveillant	*student who supervises pupils during school hours*
le tableau	*board*
le terrain de sports	*sports ground*
le travail sur bois (métal)	*woodwork (metalwork)*
les travaux pratiques (manuels) *(m.pl.)*	*craft or practical work*
un trimestre	*term*
une université	*university*
les vacances scolaires *(f.pl.)*	*school holidays*
le vestiaire	*cloakroom*

Free time (hobbies, TV, radio, reading, indoor games)

une activité	activity	le flipper	pinball machine
les actualités (f.pl.)	news	le genre	kind of
aimer	to like	un groupe	group
aimer mieux	to prefer	un jeu	game
amusant	enjoyable	un jeu de cartes	a pack of cards
s' amuser	to enjoy yourself	un jeu de société	a board game
l' argent de	pocket money		involving two
poche (m)			or more people
le babyfoot	table football		e.g. Monopoly
un ballon	ball	jouer	to play
une boum	party	jouer au bridge	to play bridge
le bricolage	craft, do-it-	jouer aux échecs	to play chess
	yourself	un journal	newspaper
une cassette	cassette	la lecture	reading
une chaîne	channel (T.V.)	libre	free
un championnat	championship	les loisirs (m.pl.)	leisure
le cinéma	cinema	un magazine	magazine
un club des jeunes	youth club	un magnétophone	tape recorder
connu	well-known	une maison des	youth centre
la couture	needlework,	jeunes	
	sewing	un match	match
la danse	dance	nager	to swim
danser	to dance	un passe-temps	hobby
un dessin animé	cartoon	la pêche	fishing
un disque	record	la peinture	painting
un documentaire	documentary	la photographie	photography
écouter	to listen to	une pièce	room
un électrophone	record player	une piscine	swimming pool
une émission	programme	la poterie	pottery
enregistrer	to record	se promener	to go for a walk
une équipe	team	la publicité	advertisements
faire une	to collect	la radio	radio
collection de	something	regarder	to watch
faire partie	to belong to	un rendez-vous	date, meeting,
d'un club	a club		appointment
faire une	to play a	un roman	novel
partie de	game of	le sport	sport
faire du théâtre	to act	une surprise-partie	party
favori	favourite	la télévision	television
un film comique	a comedy	le tricot	knitting
un film policier	a detective film	une vedette	film
un film de science-	science-fiction	le week-end	weekend
fiction	film		

Sport

un arbitre	referee
l' athlétisme (f)	athletics
le badminton	badminton
une balle	ball (for tennis, cricket etc.)
un ballon	football
le basket	basket-ball
le bowling	ten-pin bowling
les boules (f.pl.)	French-style bowls
un championnat	championship
un court de tennis	tennis court
le cyclisme	cycling
une équipe	team
l' équitation (f)	horse-riding
le football	football
le golf	golf
la gymnastique	gymnastics
le hand	hand-ball
le hockey	hockey
le jogging	jogging
jouer (à)	to play (a sport)
un joueur	player
le judo	judo
un match	match
le motocyclisme	motorcycling
la natation	swimming
le patinage	skating
la pelote	pelota (played in the Basque country)
la pétanque	French-style bowls played in the south of France)
le ping-pong	table tennis
la planche à voile	wind-surfing
le rugby	rugby
le ski (nautique)	(water) skiing
le tennis	tennis
le tennis de table	table tennis
le terrain	ground
les tribunes (f.pl.)	grandstand
la voile	sailing
le volley-ball	volleyball
le yoga	yoga

Music

l' accordéon (m)	accordeon
la batterie	percussion instruments
une chanson	song
le chant	singing
une chorale	choir
une clarinette	clarinet
un concert	concert
le conservatoire	college of music
une flûte	flute
une guitare	guitar
un harmonica	mouth organ, harmonica
un instrument de musique	musical instrument
le jazz	jazz
jouer (de)	to play (a musical instrument)
un musicien	musician
la musique classique	classical music
la musique folklorique	folk music
la musique pop	pop music
un orchestre	orchestra, band
un piano	piano
un pipeau	recorder
une trompette	trumpet
un violon	violin

9 Parts of the body

la bouche	mouth	les lèvres (f.pl.)	lips
le bras	arm	la main	hand
les cheveux (m.pl.)	hair	le menton	chin
la cheville	ankle	le nez	nose
le cœur	heart	l' œil (m)	eye(s)
le corps	body	(les yeux)	
la côte	rib	l' ongle (m)	nail
le cou	neck	les oreilles (f.pl.)	ears
le coude	elbow	l' os (m)	bone
la cuisse	thigh	la peau	skin
la dent	tooth	le pied	foot
le doigt	finger	le poignet	wrist
le doigt de pied	toe	la poitrine	chest
le dos	back	le pouce	thumb
l' épaule (f)	shoulder	le sang	blood
l' estomac (m)	stomach	le sein	breast
la figure	face	le sourcil	eyebrow
le front	forehead	la taille	waist
le genou	knee	le talon	heel
la gorge	throat	la tête	head
la hanche	hip	le ventre	stomach
la jambe	leg	le visage	face
la langue	tongue		

10 Clothing and general appearance

un anorak	anorak	une casquette	cap
assorti	matching	un chapeau	hat
avoir l'air	to seem	chauve	bald
une barbe	beard	des chaussettes (f.pl.)	socks
les bas (m.pl.)	stockings	des chaussures (f.pl.)	shoes
blond	blonde	des chaussures de ski	ski boots
un blouson	casual jacket	des chaussures de	tennis shoes
des bottes (f.pl.)	boots	tennis	
carré	square-shaped	une chemise	shirt
à carreaux	checked	une chemise de nuit	nightshirt

un chemisier	*blouse*	un manteau	*coat*
les cheveux ébouriffés *(m.pl.)*	*untidy hair*	marron	*brown*
		mince	*thin*
		la mode	*fashion*
les cheveux frisés *(m.pl.)*	*curly hair*	un mouchoir	*handkerchief*
		une moustache	*moustache*
les cheveux raides *(m.pl.)*	*straight hair*	noir	*black*
		le nylon	*nylon, synthetic material*
chic	*smart*		
le col	*collar*	un pantalon	*pair of trousers*
un collant	*tights*	un pardessus	*overcoat*
un complet	*suit*	une poche	*pocket*
le coton	*cotton*	un pullover	*pullover*
une couleur	*colour*	un pyjama	*pyjamas*
court	*short*	quelle taille?	*what size? (clothing)*
une cravate	*tie*		
le cuir	*leather*	quelle pointure?	*what size? (shoes)*
démodé	*old fashioned*		
une écharpe	*scarf*	à rayures	*striped*
un ensemble	*suit*	une robe	*dress*
étroit	*narrow*	une robe de chambre	*dressing gown*
fort	*well-built*	rond	*round*
un foulard	*scarf*	un short	*pair of shorts*
des gants *(m.pl.)*	*gloves*	un slip	*pants*
un gilet	*waistcoat*	la soie	*silk*
gris	*grey*	un soutien-gorge	*bra*
un imperméable	*raincoat*	un sweat-shirt	*sweatshirt*
un jean	*pair of jeans*	le talon	*heel*
une jupe	*skirt*	le tricot	*knitted top*
la laine	*wool*	un T-shirt	*T-shirt*
large	*wide*	uni	*single colour*
long	*long*	une veste	*jacket*
des lunettes *(f.pl.)*	*glasses*	un vêtement	*article of clothing*
un maillot de bain	*swimming costume*		

11 | At work

Professions

un(e) acteur (actrice)	*actor (actress)*	un cadre	*executive, manager*
un agent de police	*policeman*		
un boucher	*butcher*	un chauffeur de taxi	*taxi driver*
un boulanger	*baker*	un(e) coiffeur (coiffeuse)	*hairdresser*
le bureau	*office*		

un(e) concierge	*caretaker*	un(e) programmeur	*computer*
un contrôleur	*inspector*	(-euse)	*programmer*
un cuisinier	*cook*	un représentant	*representative*
un(e) dactylo	*typist*	un routier	*lorry driver*
un dentiste	*dentist*	une secrétaire	*secretary*
un(e) directeur	*head, director*	une serveuse	*waitress*
(directrice)		une sténo-dactylo	*shorthand typist*
un douanier	*customs officer*	un(e) technicien	*technician*
un électricien	*electrician*	(-enne)	
un(e) employé(e) de	*bank worker*	un(e) vendeur (-euse)	*shop assistant*
banque			
un(e) employé(e) de	*office worker*		
bureau			
un(e) employé(e) de	*railway worker*		
chemin de fer		**Useful phrases**	
un épicier	*grocer*		
un étudiant	*student*	chômage:	*to be unemployed*
un facteur	*postman*	être en ...	
un fermier	*farmer*	faire dans la vie	*to do for a*
un(e) fonctionnaire	*government*		*living*
	worker, civil	gagner sa vie	*to earn your keep*
	servant	des heures	*overtime*
un garçon de café	*waiter*	supplémentaires	
un gendarme	*policeman*	le licenciement	*redundancy*
une hôtesse de l'air	*air hostess*	un métier	*trade, job*
une hôtesse d'accueil	*receptionist*	travailler	*to work*
une infirmière	*nurse*	... dans un	*... in an office*
un ingénieur	*engineer*	bureau	
un(e) instituteur	*primary school*	... dans une usine	*... in a factory*
(institutrice)	*teacher*	... en plein air	*... outdoors*
un journaliste	*journalist*	travailler à	*to work*
un maçon	*builder*	mi-temps	*part-time*
un mécanicien	*mechanic*		
un médecin	*doctor*		
un militaire	*soldier*		
un mineur	*miner*		
un(e) ouvrier	*manual worker*		
(ouvrière)			
le patron	*boss, owner*		
un pêcheur	*fisherman*		
un pharmacien	*chemist*		
un(e) photographe	*photographer*		
un pilote	*pilot*		
un plombier	*plumber*		
un pompier	*fireman*		
un professeur	*secondary school*		
	teacher		

12 | Holidays, countries and continents

Holidays

un aéroport	airport	une glace	ice-cream
une agence de voyages	travel agency	un guide	guide-book
		un hôtel	hotel
un appareil-photo	camera	une hôtesse de l'air	air-hostess
l' argent (m)	money	le logement	board, lodgings
l' arrivée (f)	arrival	Londres	London
une assurance	insurance	louer	to hire
une auberge de jeunesse	youth hostel	des lunettes de soleil (f.pl.)	sunglasses
les bagages (m.pl.)	luggage	la Manche	the Channel
baignade interdite	bathing forbidden	la mer	sea
		le Midi	South of France
baignade surveillée	supervised bathing	la montagne	mountain
		l' office de tourisme (m)	tourist office
une brochure	brochure		
bronzer	to sunbathe, go brown	un passeport	passport
		un pays	country
la capitale	capital	une pellicule	film
une caravane	caravan	la pension (complète)	(full) board
une carte	map		
une carte postale	postcard	un pique-nique	picnic
une chaise pliante	deckchair	la plage	beach
une chambre	room	le port	port
un chèque de voyage	traveller's cheque	le propriétaire	owner
		une région	region
un circuit touristique	organised tour	le responsable	person responsible
		un sac à dos	rucksack
une colonie de vacances	children's holiday camp	un sac de couchage	sleeping bag
		un séjour	stay
un coquillage	shell	un souvenir	souvenir
les curiosités (f.pl.)	sights	un stage	course
la demi-pension	half-board	le tarif	cost, price
le départ	departure	une tente	tent
la douane	customs	se terminer	to end
un endroit	place	un terrain de camping	campsite
étranger	foreign		
à l' étranger	abroad	un(e) touriste	tourist
une excursion	trip, excursion	la traversée	crossing
la frontière	border	les (grandes) vacances (f.pl.)	(Summer) holidays
un gîte	holiday country home		
		une valise	suitcase

une visite guidée	guided tour
visiter	to visit
voler	to fly
le voyage	journey
voyager	to travel
un voyageur	traveller

Main public holidays

la fête nationale	national holiday
le jour de l'An	New Year's Day
mardi gras	Shrove Tuesday
Noël	Christmas
Pâques	Easter
la Pentecôte	Whitsun
la Toussaint	All Saints' day

le Maroc	Morocco
la Norvège	Norway
la Nouvelle Zélande	New Zealand
le pays de Galles	Wales
la Pologne	Poland
le Portugal	Portugal
la Russie	Russia
la Suède	Sweden
la Suisse	Switzerland
la Tunisie	Tunisia
la Yougoslavie	Yugoslavia

Countries and continents

l' Afrique (f)	Africa
l' Allemagne (f)	Germany
l' Amérique du nord (f)	North America
l' Amérique du sud (f)	South America
l' Angleterre (f)	England
l' Asie (f)	Asia
l' Australie (f)	Australia
l' Autriche (f)	Austria
la Belgique	Belgium
le Canada	Canada
la Chine	China
le Danemark	Denmark
l' Écosse (f)	Scotland
l' Espagne (f)	Spain
les États-Unis (m.pl.)	United States
l' Europe (f)	Europe
la France	France
la Grèce	Greece
la Hollande	Holland
l' Irlande (f)	Ireland
l' Irlande du nord	Northern Ireland
l' Italie (f)	Italy
le Japon	Japan
le Luxembourg	Luxembourg

À bientôt	*See you soon*	
À ce soir (à demain)	*See you this evening (...tomorrow)*	
À tout à l'heure	*See you later*	
accepter	*to accept*	
l' adresse *(f)*	*address*	
un ami	*friend*	
amicalement ⎤	*best wishes* (end	
amitiés ⎦	of a letter)	
au revoir	*goodbye*	
(très) bien	*(very) well*	
une bise	*a kiss*	
Bon voyage!	*Have a good journey!*	
bonjour	*good morning, hello*	
bonne nuit	*good night*	
bonsoir	*good evening*	
un cadeau	*present*	
un(e) camarade	*colleague*	
ça va?	*how are you?*	
célibataire	*single*	
cher	*dear*	
chez	*at (someone's house)*	
un(e) collègue	*colleague*	
comment?	*pardon?*	
connaître	*to know, be acquainted with*	
un(e) copain (copine)	*friend*	
un correspondant	*penfriend*	
d'accord	*OK, agreed*	
de rien	*it's nothing*	
déranger	*to disturb*	
dérangez: Ne vous...pas.	*Don't go to any trouble*	
désolé	*very sorry*	
D'où venez-vous?	*Where are you from?*	
enchanté	*pleased to meet you*	
épeler	*to spell*	
excusez-moi	*I'm sorry; excuse me*	

faire la connaissance	*to get to know*	
la famille	*family*	
félicitations	*congratulations*	
c'est (très) gentil	*it's (very) kind*	
heureux	*happy*	
inquiétez: Ne vous...pas.	*Don't worry.*	
une invitation	*invitation*	
inviter	*to invite*	
Je ne comprends pas.	*I don't understand*	
libre	*free*	
marié	*married*	
meilleurs vœux	*best wishes*	
merci (beaucoup)	*thanks (very much)*	
le nom	*name*	
non	*no*	
le numéro de téléphone	*telephone number*	
offrir	*to give*	
oui	*yes*	
pardon	*I'm sorry*	
les parents	*parents*	
parlez plus lentement	*speak more slowly*	
permettre	*to allow*	
un plaisir	*pleasure*	
le prénom	*Christian name*	
se présenter	*to introduce oneself*	
refuser	*to refuse*	
regretter	*to be sorry*	
remercier	*to thank*	
rencontrer	*to meet*	
un rendez-vous	*an appointment*	
répéter	*to repeat*	
salut!	*hello; hi!*	
un sentiment	*feeling*	
s'il vous plaît	*please*	
sympa(thique)	*nice*	
un veuf	*widower*	
une veuve	*widow*	
un voisin	*neighbour*	

abominable	ghastly	idiot	stupid
adorer	to love	inquiet	anxious
affreux	dreadful	insupportable	insufferable
agréable	pleasant	intéressant	interesting
aimable	kind, nice	jaloux	jealous
aimer	to like	laid	ugly
l' amour	love	magnifique	superb
amusant	enjoyable, fun	malheureux	unhappy
un avis	opinion	malin	clever
à mon avis	in my opinion	marrant	funny, amusing
à ton (votre) avis	in your opinion	méchant	naughty, spiteful
bien	well	mince!	blow!
bizarre	odd, peculiar	moche	rotten, ugly
une blague	joke	oh là là!	goodness!
Bof!	So what? (implies indifference)	pas mal	not bad
		pas tellement	not much
c'est ça	that's right	penser de	to think of
le chagrin	grief, suffering	la peur	fear
chic alors!	great!	peur: avoir...	to be afraid
chouette	fine	pleurer	to cry
content	happy	préférer	to prefer
craindre	to fear	rire	to laugh
désagréable	unpleasant	quelle horreur!	what a mess!
détester	to hate	scandale: c'est un ...!	it's scandalous!
c'est dommage	it's a pity		
entendu	agreed, understood	sensationnel	great, terrific!
		sourire	to smile
épatant	great	sympathique	nice
épouvantable	dreadful	tant mieux	so much the better
un espoir	hope		
être en colère	to be angry	tant pis	too bad
excellent	excellent	triste	sad
se fâcher	to get angry	vilain	nasty
(pas) fameux	(not) very good	zut!	blast!
fantastique	fantastic		
Fichez-moi la paix!	Clear off!		
fier	proud		
formidable	terrific		
franchement	frankly		
honte: avoir...	to be ashamed		
horrible	horrid		
bonne idée	good idea		

acheter	to buy
une alimentation générale	general food shop
l' argent (m)	money
un ascenseur	lift
un billet	bank note; ticket
bon marché	cheap
une boucherie	butcher's
une boulangerie	baker's
une boutique	small shop; boutique
un bureau de tabac	tobacconist
une cabine d'essayage	changing room, cubicle
la caisse	cash desk; check out
une charcuterie	pork butcher's; delicatessen
un chariot	supermarket trolley
cher	expensive, dear
chercher	to look for
un client	customer
combien?	how much?
un commerçant	shopkeeper
confection dames	ladies' ready to wear clothing
confection hommes	men's ready to wear clothing
une confiserie	confectioner's
coûter	to cost
une crèmerie	dairy
dépenser	to spend
désirer	to want
une droguerie	general household shop
l' entrée	entrance
"entrée libre"	'no obligation to buy'
une épicerie	grocer's
essayer	to try
faire des économies	to save
faire du lèche-vitrine	to go window-shopping
faire un paquet-cadeau	to gift wrap
fermé	closed
un flacon	small bottle
un grand magasin	department store
les heures d'ouverture (f.pl.)	opening hours
un kiosque	kiosk
une librairie	bookshop
libre-service	self-service
un magasin	shop
la maison de la presse	newsagent
un marché	market
la monnaie	change
montrer	to show
ouvert	open
une papeterie	stationer's
une pâtisserie	cake shop
payer	to pay
une pharmacie	chemist
chez le photographe	at the photographer's
prendre	to take
le prix	price
une quincaillerie	ironmonger's, hardware shop
le rayon	department; shelf
recommander	to recommend
regarder	to look at, watch
une solde	sale bargain
la sortie	exit
un supermarché	supermarket
les surgelés (m.pl.)	frozen food
un traiteur	delicatessen; pork butcher
la T.V.A.	V.A.T.
un(e) vendeur (vendeuse)	shop assistant
vendre	to sell
la vitrine	shop window
vouloir	to want

des allumettes *(f.pl.)*	*matches*		du rouge à lèvres	*lipstick*
une balle	*ball (small)*		un sac à main	*handbag*
un ballon	*ball (large)*		le savon	*soap*
un bic	*biro*		le scotch	*Sellotape*
un bouquet de fleurs	*bunch of flowers*		les serviettes	*sanitary towels*
une brosse à dents	*toothbrush*		hygiéniques	
un cahier	*exercise book*		*(f.pl.)*	
une calculatrice	*calculator*		du shampooing	*shampoo*
un carnet	*notebook*		un stylo	*pen*
une carte	*map*		un tire-bouchon	*corkscrew*
une carte postale	*postcard*			
une cassette	*cassette*			
des ciseaux *(m.pl.)*	*scissors*			
de la colle	*glue*			
un crayon	*pencil*			
une crème solaire	*suntan cream*			
le démaquillage	*make-up remover*			
le dentifrice	*toothpaste*			
un disque	*record*			
une enveloppe	*envelope*			
un guide	*guide book*			
un jouet	*toy*			
un journal	*newspaper*			
une lampe de poche	*torch*			
la lessive	*washing powder*			
le liquide pour la	*washing-up*			
vaisselle	*liquid*			
un livre	*book*			
des lunettes de soleil	*sunglasses*			
le maquillage	*make-up*			
un mouchoir	*(paper) hanky*			
(en papier)				
une montre	*watch*			
un ouvre-boîtes	*tin opener*			
du papier (à écrire)	*(writing) paper*			
du papier hygiénique	*toilet paper*			
du parfum	*perfume*			
un parapluie	*umbrella*			
un peigne	*comb*			
une pelle	*spade*			
une pellicule	*film*			
des piles *(f.pl.)*	*batteries*			
un roman	*novel*			

17 | Food and drink

un abricot	apricot	le jambon	ham
l' agneau (m)	lamb	le jus de fruit	fruit juice
l' ail (m)	garlic	le lait	milk
un ananas	pineapple	une laitue	lettuce
un artichaut	artichoke	le lapin	rabbit
une aubergine	aubergine	un légume	vegetable
une banane	banana	la limonade	lemonade
le beurre	butter	la mayonnaise	mayonnaise
une bière	beer	un melon	melon
le bifteck	steak	la moutarde	mustard
le bœuf	beef	un œuf	egg
une boisson	drink	un oignon	onion
le café	coffee	une omelette	omelette
le canard	duck	une orange	orange
une carotte	carrot	l' Orangina (m)	fizzy orangeade
une cerise	cherry	le pain	bread
un champignon	mushroom	un pamplemousse	grapefruit
de la charcuterie	cold cooked meats, e.g. ham	le pâté	pâté
		les pâtes (f.pl.)	pasta
le chocolat	chocolate	une pêche	peach
un chou	cabbage	le persil	parsley
un chou-fleur	cauliflower	les petits pois (m.pl.)	peas
le cidre	cider	une poire	pear
un citron	lemon	le poisson	fish
le Coca-cola	coca cola	le poivre	pepper
un concombre	cucumber	un poivron	green pepper
une courgette	courgette	une pomme	apple
la crème	cream	une pomme de terre	potato
un croissant	croissant	le porc	pork
les crudités (f.pl.)	raw, chopped vegetables	le potage	soup
		le poulet	chicken
l' eau (f)	water	une prune	plum
l' eau minérale	mineral water	une quiche	small savoury tart
une fraise	strawberry	les radis (m.pl.)	radishes
une framboise	raspberry	le raisin	grape
les frites (f.pl.)	chips	un rôti de bœuf	roast beef
le fromage	cheese	la salade	green salad
un fruit	piece of fruit	le salami	salami
une glace	ice cream	un sandwich	sandwich
les haricots verts (m.pl.)	green beans	les sardines (f.pl.)	sardines
		la sauce	sauce, gravy
l' huile (f)	oil	une saucisse	sausage

un saucisson	*spicy, continental sausage*	le thé	*tea*
le saumon	*salmon*	une tomate	*tomato*
le sel	*salt*	la truite	*trout*
la soupe	*soup*	le veau	*veal*
le sucre	*sugar*	la viande	*meat*
une tarte	*tart*	le vin	*wine*

---

18 │ Eating out

à point	*medium cooked (steak)*	excellent	*excellent*
l' addition *(f)*	*bill*	une fourchette	*fork*
un apéritif	*aperitif*	frais	*fresh*
une assiette	*plate*	fumer	*to smoke*
avoir faim	*to be hungry*	le garçon	*waiter*
avoir soif	*to be thirsty*	goûter	*to waste*
bien cuit	*well done (steak)*	le goûter	*afternoon tea*
un bistro	*small restaurant*	un hors-d'œuvre	*starter, first course*
boire	*to drink*	léger	*light*
une boisson	*drink*	manger	*to eat*
bon	*good*	le menu (à prix fixe)	*(fixed-price) menu*
Bon appétit!	*Enjoy your meal!*	la nourriture	*food*
un bouchon	*cork*	une pâtisserie	*pastry, cake*
un café	*cup of coffee, café*	le plat du jour	*today's special dish*
une carafe	*carafe*	le plat principal	*main course*
la carte	*menu*	un plateau	*tray*
le chef	*chef*	une portion	*portion*
choisir	*to choose*	un pourboire	*tip*
au choix	*choice of*	prendre	*to have, take*
un client	*customer*	un restaurant	*restaurant*
commander	*to order*	de saison	*in season*
en conserve	*tinned*	une serveuse	*waitress*
un couteau	*knife*	le service	*service charge*
le couvert	*table setting, cover charge*	service compris	*service charge included*
une cuillère	*spoon*	servir	*to serve*
dégoûtant	*disgusting*	du sirop	*squash*
le déjeuner	*lunch*	la terrasse	*terrace*
délicieux	*delicious*	une tranche	*slice*
le dessert	*dessert, sweet*		
le dîner	*dinner*		

un aéroglisseur	hovercraft	la direction	direction
un aéroport	airport	le document	document
une agence de voyages	travel agency	durer	to last
		enregistrer	to register
un aller-retour	return ticket	une excursion	excursion
un aller simple	single ticket	un express	regional train
s' arrêter	to stop	faire de l'auto-stop	to hitch-hike
un arrêt d'autobus	bus stop		
l' arrière (f)	rear, back	la fenêtre	window
arriver	to arrive	fermer	to close
un autobus	bus	le ferry	ferry
un autocar	coach	les feux (m.pl.)	traffic lights
l' auto-stop (m)	hitch-hiking	la gare	station
un avion	plane	la gare routière	bus or coach station
les bagages (m.pl.)	luggage		
la barrière	barrier	le guichet	booking office
un bateau	boat	les heures d'affluence (f.pl.)	rush hour
une bicyclette	bicycle		
un billet	ticket		
le bureau de renseignements	information office	l' horaire (m)	timetable
		une hôtesse de l'air	air hostess
le car	coach	le hovercraft	hovercraft
un carnet	book of métro tickets	interdit	forbidden
		un kilomètre	kilometre
la ceinture de sécurité	safety belt	lent	slow
		lentement	slowly
changer	to change	libre	free
le chauffeur	driver	la ligne	line
le chemin	way	le machiniste	bus driver
le chemin de fer	railway	le mal de l'air (de mer)	travel (sea) sickness
un compartiment	compartment		
composter	to date stamp a ticket	manquer	to miss
		la mer	sea
la consigne	left luggage	le métro	métro
la correspondance	connection	monter	to get on
une couchette	sleeping berth	une moto	motor bike
un cycliste	cyclist	non-fumeurs	non-smoking
défense de	forbidden to	normal	normal, regular
le départ	departure	le numéro	number
dernier	last	obligatoire	compulsory
descendre	to get off	à pied	on foot
(en) deuxième classe	(by) second class	un piéton	pedestrian
direct	direct	une place	place

un porteur	porter	un taxi	taxi
premier	first	terminer	to end
prochain	next	le train	train
le quai	platform	le trajet	journey
quitter	to leave	traverser	to cross
un rapide	express inter-city train	valable	valid
		une valise	case
le receveur	conductor	un vélo	bicycle
réserver	to reserve	un vélomoteur	moped
en retard	late	vite	quickly
le retour	return journey	la voie	platform
une salle d'attente	waiting room	la voiture	car
la SNCF	French Railways	un vol	flight
la sortie	exit	le voyage	journey
une station de métro	metro station	un voyageur	traveller
un supplément	supplement	le wagon-restaurant	dining car

---

20 | Travelling by car

un accident (de route)	(road) accident	un(e) conducteur (conductrice)	driver
l' air	air	conduire	to drive
s' arrêter	to stop	en contravention	in breach of the law
une assurance	insurance		
un(e) automobiliste	car driver	dangereux	dangerous
une autoroute	motorway	défense de	forbidden to
la batterie	car battery	déraper	to skid
un bidon d'huile	can of oil	une déviation	diversion
un bouchon	bottle-neck, traffic jam	la direction	direction
		doubler	to overtake
un bruit	noise	l' eau (f)	water
un camion	lorry	un embouteillage	traffic jam
une camionette	van	l' essence (f)	petrol
casser	to break	essuyer	to wipe
une ceinture de sécurité	seat belt	les essuie-glaces (m)	windscreen wipers
		l' état (m)	state
changer	to change	éteindre	to extinguish
la circulation	traffic	faire un constat	to make a report (after an accident)
le code de la route	highway code		
le coffre	boot		

faire le plein	to fill up with petrol	stationner	to park
les feux (m.pl.)	traffic lights	super	4 star petrol
frapper	to hit	un témoin	witness
freiner	to brake	toutes directions	all directions
les freins (m.pl.)	brakes	les travaux (m.pl.)	road works
le garage	garage	un trou	hole
garer	to park	le verglas	black ice
un gendarme	policeman	vérifier	to check
l' huile (f)	oil	un virage	bend
un instrument	instrument	la vitesse	speed
le klaxon	horn	une voie piétonne	pedestrian precinct
klaxonner	to sound the horn	une voiture	car
un litre	litre	le volant	steering wheel
marcher	to work		
la marque	make		
le mécanicien	mechanic		
le moteur	engine		
le numéro d'immatriculation	registration number		
ordinaire	ordinary (2-star petrol)		
en panne	broken down		
les papiers (m.pl.)	papers		
le pare-brise	windscreen		
un parking	car park		
un passage à niveau	level crossing		
le permis de conduire	driving licence		
les phares (m.pl.)	headlights		
un piéton	pedestrian		
un pneu (crevé)	(burst) tyre		
un poids lourd	heavy goods lorry		
une portière	car door		
la pression	pressure		
la priorité	priority		
le radiateur	radiator		
ralentir	to slow down		
le rétroviseur	rear-view mirror		
les réparations (f.pl.)	repairs		
une roue de secours	spare wheel		
rouler	to drive		
la route	road		
la route nationale	main road, 'A' road		
sens unique	one-way traffic		
une station-service	petrol station		

l' adresse (f)	address	la ligne	line
allô	hello (when	la livre sterling	pound sterling
	answering	un mandat-lettre	postal order,
	phone)		money order
l' annuaire	telephone	un message	message
téléphonique	directory	la monnaie	change
(m)		le numéro de	phone number
l' appareil (m)	machine, phone	téléphone	
un appel	telephone call	ne quittez pas!	hold on
téléphonique		occupé	engaged
l' argent (m)	money	par avion	by air mail
attendre	to wait	un paquet	parcel
une banque	bank	un passeport	passport
un billet	bank note, ticket	en P.C.V.	reverse charges
une boîte à lettres	letter box	une pièce d'identité	form of
un bureau de change	exchange office		identification
une cabine	booth	la poste	post office
la caisse	cash desk	le poste	extension number
changer	to change	poste restante	department in
un chèque	cheque		main post
un chèque de	traveller's		office where
voyage	cheque		letters are kept
un colis	parcel		until called for
le courrier	post	raccròcher	to replace the
le cours de change	exchange rate		receiver,
la devise	currency		hang up
écouter	to listen	rappeler	to call back
écrire	to write	un récepteur	receiver
enregistrer	to register	un reçu	receipt
entendre	to hear	remplir	to fill in
une enveloppe	envelope	des renseignements	information
envoyer	to send	(m.pl.)	
un facteur	postman	répondre	to reply
un formulaire	printed form	sonner	to ring
le franc français	French (Belgian,	la signature	signature
(belge, suisse)	Swiss) franc	signer	to sign
le guichet	counter	le tarif normal	ordinary
des imprimés (m.pl.)	printed matter	(réduit)	(reduced) rate
un jeton	token (for use	un télégramme	telegram
	with older style	le téléphone	telephone
	automatic	un timbre	stamp
	telephones)	toucher un	to cash a cheque
une lettre	letter	chèque	
la levée	collection	utiliser	to use

un abonnement	season ticket	gagner	to win
un(e) acteur (actrice)	actor (actress)	gratuit	free of charge
une affiche	notice	un groupe	group
l' ambiance (f)	atmosphere	l' heure (f)	time, hour
l' arbitre (m)	referee, umpire	une histoire	story
le bal	dance	l' horaire (m)	schedule, timing
le balcon	circle (cinema, theatre)	un joueur	player
		la location	hire, booking (of seats)
le ballet	ballet		
un billet	ticket	un match	match
une boîte de nuit	nightclub	une matinée	afternoon performance
un but	goal		
la caisse	ticket office	un musée	museum
célèbre	famous	l' opéra (m)	opera
un cinéma	cinema	l' orchestre (m)	stalls
un cirque	circus	l' ouvreuse (f)	usherette
comique	amusing, comedy	une patinoire	skating rink
le commencement	beginning	une place	place
commencer	to begin	un pourboire	tip
un concert	concert	un programme	programme
une course de taureaux	bull fight	un rideau	curtain
		une séance	performance
un cowboy	cowboy	la science-fiction	science fiction
des curiosités (f.pl.)	sights	une soirée (folklorique)	(folk) evening
un dessin animé	cartoon		
une discothèque	disco	la sortie	exit
une distraction	amusement, form of entertainment	sous-titré	sub-titled
		un spectacle "Son et Lumière"	'Son et Lumière' show
un documentaire	documentary	le tarif	price
l' écran (m)	screen	un théâtre	theatre
l' entracte (f)	interval	une vedette	film star
l' entrée (f)	entrance	en version originale	in the original version
une exposition	exhibition		
un festival	festival	un zoo	zoo
une fête foraine	funfair		
un feu d'artifice	firework display		
un film (policier)	(detective) film		
la fin	end		
finir	to finish		

Zoo or circus animals

un crocodile	crocodile	un loup	wolf
un éléphant	elephant	un rhinocéros	rhinoceros
une girafe	giraffe	un serpent	snake
un gorille	gorilla	un singe	monkey
un guépard	cheetah	un tigre	tiger
un hippopotame	hippopotamus	un zèbre	zebra
un lion	lion		

---

23 | Holiday accommodation (hotel, campsite etc.)

à partir de	from	la demi-pension	half board
l' accueil (m)	reception desk	le départ	departure
s' adresser à	to refer to, to report to	descendre (à un hôtel)	to stay (at a hotel)
annuler	to cancel	un dortoir	dormitory
l' arrivée (f)	arrival	une douche	shower
un ascenseur	lift	les draps (m.pl.)	sheets
une auberge de jeunesse	youth hostel	l' eau chaude (f)	hot water
		l' eau froide (f)	cold water
un balcon	balcony	l' eau potable (f)	drinking water
un bidet	bidet	un emplacement	site
le bloc sanitaire	washrooms	un endroit	place
le bureau	office	une erreur	mistake
un cabinet de toilette	washing facilities	un escalier	staircase
		un étage	storey
un camping	campsite	un évier	sink
une caravane	caravan	la facture	bill
une carte d'adhérant	membership card	une fiche	note, form
casser	to break	un gardien	warden
une chambre	room	le gaz	gas
un champ	field	un gîte	self-catering accommodation (usually in the country)
le chauffage central	central heating		
le chauffe-eau	water heater		
un cintre	coat hanger		
une clé	key	un hôtel	hotel
complet	full	installer	to settle in
le confort	comfort	un lavabo	washbasin
une couverture	blanket	libre	free
la date	date	le linge	linen

un lit	bed	un repas	meal
un locataire	tenant	réserver	to reserve
le logement	lodging	rester	to stay
le loyer	rent	le rez-de-chaussée	ground floor
la lumière	light	le robinet	tap
manger	to eat	un sac à dos	rucksack
marcher	to work (of a machine)	un sac de couchage	sleeping bag
		la salle à manger	dining room
le nom	name	la salle de bains	bathroom
la note	bill	le salon	lounge
la nuit	night	le savon	soap
le numéro	number	un séjour	stay
occupé	engaged	une semaine	week
à l' ombre	in the shade	le service	service
un oreiller	pillow	une serviette	towel
un passeport	passport	signer	to sign
la pension complète	full board	sonner	to ring
une personne	person	une table	table
la pièce	room	le tarif	price
une pièce d'identité	form of identification	une tente	tent
		un terrain de camping	campsite
une poubelle	dustbin	les toilettes	toilets
un propriétaire	owner	les vacances (f.pl.)	holidays
une prise d'électricité	electric point	une valise	suitcase
la réception	reception area	une voiture	car
un reçu	receipt	les W.C.	W.C.
des renseignements (m.pl.)	information		

24 | Illness or injury

un accident	accident	le cabinet de médecin	doctor's consulting room
une ambulance	ambulance		
une ampoule	blister		
une angine	sore throat	se casser (la jambe etc)	to break (one's leg etc.)
appeler	to call		
l' aspirine (f)	aspirin	à cause de	because of
avaler	to swallow	le chirurgien	surgeon
aveugle	blind	la clinique	hospital
être blessé	to be injured	les comprimés (m.pl.)	tablets
blesser	to injure		
se brûler	to get burnt	conseiller	to advise

la constipation	constipation	un pansement	dressing
le coton	cotton wool	des pastilles (f.pl.)	throat sweets
un coup de soleil	sunstroke	la peau	skin
une crampe	cramp	une pharmacie	chemist
une crème	cream	un pharmacien	chemist
une crise cardiaque	heart attack	la pilule	pill
une crise de nerfs	nervous breakdown	une piqûre	injection
		le plâtre	plaster
dangereux	dangerous	un plombage	filling
une dent	tooth	prendre	to take
le dentiste	dentist	un problème	problem
se déshabiller	to get undressed	la radio	X-ray
la diarrhée	diaorrhea	les règles (f.pl.)	period
le docteur	doctor	un rendez-vous	appointment
dormir	to sleep	se reposer	to rest
la douleur	pain	rester	to stay
être enrhumé	to have a cold	le sang	blood
une entorse	sprain	la santé	health
examiner	to examine	(se) sentir	to feel
faible	weak	du secours	help
fatigué	tired	sévère	serious
fièvre: avoir de la ...	to have a temperature	signer	to sign
		soigner	to care for
frotter	to rub	souffrir	to suffer
les gouttes (f.pl.)	drops	du sparadrap	Elastoplast
grave	serious	un suppositoire	suppository
la grippe	flu	la température	temperature
les heures de consultation (f.pl.)	surgery hours	tomber	to fall
		tousser	to cough
		tranquille	calm
l' hôpital (m)	hospital	trembler	to shake, shiver
une infirmière	nurse	triste	sad
inquiet	anxious	urgent	urgent
un lit	bed	la vignette	special tax label on drugs bought at chemist
le mal de l'air	air-sickness		
le mal de mer	sea-sickness		
avoir mal à	to be in pain		
malade	ill		
un(e) malade	patient		
une maladie	disease		
le médecin	doctor		
un médicament	medication		
mort	dead		
mourir	to die		
nécessaire	necessary		
une ordonnance	prescription		
l' os (m)	bone		

25 | Problems (lost property, complaints, theft)

un accident (de route)	(road) accident	une gendarmerie	police station
l' adresse (f)	address	un incendie	fire
les affaires (f.pl.)	things	inutile	pointless
une aiguille	needle	laisser	to leave
l' alarme (f)	alarm	manquer	to miss
apercevoir	to notice	ne marche plus	is no longer working
appeler	to call	marqué(e) à mon	marked with my
l' argent (m)	money	nom	name
attention!	watch out!	mettre	to put
des bagages (m.pl.)	luggage	un mot	word, note
bouché	blocked	le nom	name
le bureau des objets trouvés	lost property office	un notaire	solicitor
casser	to break	nouveau	new
chercher	to look for	nulle part	nowhere
coincé	caught, wedged, jammed	où	where
le commissariat de police	police station	oublier	to forget
le consulat britannique	British consul	un paquet	parcel
déchirer	to tear	pas du tout	not at all
découvrir	to discover	satisfait(e)	satisfied
un défaut	fault	perdre	to lose
une description	description	se plaindre de	to complain
disparaître	to disappear	la police	the police
se disputer	to argue	un porte-feuille	wallet
donner l'alerte	to sound the alarm	un porte-monnaie	purse
échanger	to change	quand	when
épeler	to spell	une récompense	reward
une épingle (de sûreté)	(safety) pin	(me) rembourser	to refund (my money)
épouvantable	dreadful	remercier	to thank
une erreur	mistake	réparer	to repair
expliquer	to explain	répéter	to repeat
la faute	fault	retrouver	to find again
(au) feu!	fire!	sale	dirty
une fiche	form, note	les sapeurs-pompiers (m.pl.)	fire service
du fil	thread	sembler	to seem
garder	to keep	se tromper	to make a mistake
un gendarme	policeman	trouver	to find
		vieux	old
		voler	to steal
		un voleur	thief

Index to Grammar Section